FROM BONDAGE TO FREEDOM

How I Broke Free from a Spirit Spouse Using 7 Biblical Keys

By
Sharon Mbi

ACKNOWLEDGMENTS

To my beloved **husband**, you are my partner in this journey of life, and I am endlessly grateful to you.

Aiden, thank you for believing in the 7 songs before they were sung and giving them form with your piano gift before they were officially produced.

Chloe, your keen eye and tender heart shaped this book, from editing its raw pages sometimes with me to helping me choose a title. Thank you.

Ira, when weariness draped itself over me as I labored on this book, you'd slip into my space, your hug a quiet roar that said, "You've got this, Mom."

To my sister-in-law **Kim**, you saw the story in me before I dared to dream it, urging me to pour the Seven Songs from Heaven into these pages. Thank you.

Thank you to all of you who offered support during the very beginning of this journey, even when things were unclear. Your presence helped me take my first steps, and for that, I'm grateful.

Copyright © 2025 by Sharon Mbi

ISBN: 979-8-218-71590-8

Copyright & Disclaimer Note

Scripture quotations are taken from the Holy Bible, New International Version® (NIV®). Copyright © 1973, 1978, 1984, 2011 by Biblica, Inc. ™ Used by permission. All rights reserved worldwide.

This book is a work of testimony, biblical teaching, and spiritual insight, written to encourage and equip individuals on their journey of healing and deliverance through Christ. While it may be used as a resource in pastoral care and ministry settings, it is not intended to replace personal discipleship, local church leadership, or professional counseling where needed.

DEDICATION

To my beloved children, Aiden, Chloe, and Ira.

You became my most outstanding teachers from the moment you entered my life. Your presence sparked a fire in me, a resolve to break chains in Jesus' name.

Table of Contents

CHAPTER I

INTRODUCTION

From a tender age, I began to experience the terrifying symptoms associated with a spirit husband. As I transitioned into my teenage years and early adulthood, these oppressive manifestations escalated. Nightmares, sleep paralysis, and relentless lustful dreams plagued me. Initially, the dreams seemed pleasurable, but when I started to resist, I felt as if I was being violated in my sleep. Nighttime became a period of overwhelming oppression and unrest, trapping me in a cycle of fear.

By my early twenties, the weight of this demonic activity had ensnared me in a vicious cycle of anxiety, panic disorder, and rejection. It was during this tumultuous period that I began to comprehend the impact of "family of origin narcissistic abuse." Though I loved Jesus, I realized I had been introduced to a distorted version of Him. I was raised under a distorted expression of Christianity, one that emphasized fear, control, and religious performance over a relationship with God. Behind the surface of religion, there were spiritual practices and strongholds rooted in manipulation and, unknowingly, even witchcraft. This spiritual atmosphere opened doors that led to deep bondage, including the spirit spouse. I believe many of those in authority were doing what they knew or what had been passed down to them generationally. But the impact of that spiritual foundation created deep confusion in my soul and opened doors to the demonic influence that I later had to confront through deliverance.

I was determined to break free from the control of narcissism. In my confusion, the enemy placed the wrong people in my life, introducing me to horoscopes, pornography, and Eastern meditation. While I initially found relief, it was a false sense of peace, leading me deeper into a pit of despair. The symptoms worsened; I struggled through school, receiving incompletes in most of my classes, and my fiancé eventually left me, unable to bear the turmoil within me.

However, God was persistent. After my fiancé's departure, He embarked on a journey with me that would last well into my mid-thirties to reintroduce Himself. It is far easier to introduce Jesus to someone who has never known Him than to someone like me, who has encountered a perverted representation of His love. But through gentle nudges, I began to seek churches that embraced the ministry of the Holy Spirit and understood spiritual warfare. I started asking for forgiveness for any occult involvement, not just for myself but for past generations. I committed to fasting and declaring the Word of God over my life. This new era of spiritual warfare offered a measure of freedom; I returned to school, earned my degree, and secured a job as a psychiatric registered nurse. In a remarkable twist, my fiancé returned to me, and we married. Yet, after our wedding, the spirit spouse manifested in new ways, impacting our intimacy and causing my husband to withdraw from church, leading to disunity in our marriage. My desire for children grew, and we attempted to conceive, but it felt impossible. I knew the spirit spouse was at work, so I fervently prayed to Jesus, claiming His promises in Psalms 113, asking Him to make the barren woman a joyful mother of children.

Miraculously, despite our struggles, Jesus granted us the miracle of conception. Later, doctors told us I was born with only one ovary and a twisted fallopian tube, a condition known as tubal torsion, which significantly reduces the chances of natural conception. Medically, they said I should not have been able to conceive any of my children, but by God's grace, I did. During my pregnancy, the spirit spouse threatened me in dreams, vowing death and warning me that my son would be autistic. I battled pre-eclampsia and severe sickness while also grappling with postpartum anxiety, which left me over-whelmed and even contemplating suicide. It felt as though the demon was winning.

In time, I conceived two more children who exhibited seizures and strange infirmities. After my third child's birth, I nearly lost my life due to postpartum hemorrhaging, all the while knowing these events were tied to the spirit spouse's threats in my dreams, threats that would often come to pass. Through this harrowing experience, I clung tightly to God. I prayed fervently, I had triumphed over barrenness through Christ, yet the dark forces continued their relentless attacks, often rendering me unable to care for my own children, necessitating frequent emergency visits for unidentifiable symptoms.

I lived many days helplessly on my couch, crying out to God, while my husband rushed home from work to care for our children. Until that point, I had concealed my battle with the evil spirit spouse from everyone, including my husband, feeling immense shame and embarrassment. Growing up in a religious home only deepened my reluctance to share. Meanwhile, my husband would spend Sundays watching football or picking up extra shifts at work while I was at church, fasting and praying.

Finally, the Holy Spirit urged me to forsake my shame and pride. He gave me the courage to seek deliverance prayer from a pastor and, most importantly, to open up to my husband. Sharing my struggles with him, despite our ongoing disunity, marked a pivotal turning point toward deeper freedom. However, the road was not easy. My husband initially reacted with disgust, unable to fathom that an evil spirit could claim me as its wife. Our conversation led to yet another fight, and I returned to the Lord, crying out in despair, feeling as if I had misunderstood His guidance. But God, who values unity in marriage, was indeed behind my decision to share. Days later, the spirit spouse threatened my husband in a dream, revealing that it had been behind much of our turmoil. This revelation ignited a righteous anger in him, transforming his passivity into spiritual warfare. His disgust was replaced by compassion and love, igniting a desire to fight for our family.

The turning point in my journey came during a season of deep worship. I wasn't looking for a formula; I was just seeking God. But as I spent time in His presence, singing songs that rose up from my spirit, He began revealing seven spiritual keys through those melodies. Each one became an invitation to study His Word more deeply. God showed me that these keys, love, joy, worship, grace, warfare, faith, and freedom; were not just theological concepts. They were weapons. These songs are available for you to download and listen to on all streaming platforms.

I began to intentionally apply these seven keys to my own character and daily habits. I studied what the Bible said about each one. I repented where I had lived contrary to them. I replaced toxic generational patterns with kingdom truth, and that's when everything began to change. My dreams shifted. My mind became clear. I felt safe in my own skin again; I began serving with my God-given gifts and talents, and I knew without a doubt that the spirit spouse had lost its hold on me. My husband stepped into his role as the spiritual leader of our home, a role I had longed for and prayed for; for years. He began to pray and fast for me and our children, a practice he continues to this day. We began taking communion nightly, claiming our covenant with Christ, renouncing all other covenants associated with Satan, and commanding the dark forces to leave our family in Jesus' name.

The strange infirmities that plagued me and our children vanished, and the heavy darkness that had once rested upon our home lifted. We are now united spiritually, and we serve God together joyfully, having created a worship space in our community called Worship War Win Sessions, which are held yearly here in southern California, where we address the issues we've faced and bring hope to others. Glory to God!

CHAPTER 2

Understanding Spirit Spouses

The first step in overcoming a problem is to identify exactly what the problem is. In order to overcome the assault of the spirit spouse upon your life, you must first understand what a spirit spouse is, how it enters the lives of those whom it oppresses, and how it operates. Spirit spouses are demonic spirits. They are usually referred to as spiritual husbands or spiritual wives. These beings, including the **incubus spirit** (manifests as a male demonic entity) and the **succubus spirit** (manifests as a female demonic entity). They usually appear in people's dreams as sexual partners and are part of a calculated assault by Satan to destroy godly homes, sabotage relationships, and derail lives. Their goal is to rob people of their peace, joy, purpose, and connection with God. But despite their cunning and persistence, spirit spouses are not invincible. **The power of God is infinitely greater than any force of darkness**. Through faith, prayer, and the authority of Jesus Christ, their influence can be completely dismantled. Recognizing their presence is the first step in breaking free from their hold. The Word of God is a powerful weapon, for it exposes their lies and brings light into the darkness where they operate.

Is the Concept of a Spirit Spouse Biblical?

The concept of a spirit spouse is not only real but also deeply rooted in Scripture. All born-again believers are spiritually married to Christ, our true spirit spouse. Ephesians 5:25-27 commands husbands to love their wives as Christ loved the church, highlighting the sacred marriage-like bond between Christ and His followers. In Revelation 19:7-9, we witness the joyous proclamation of the wedding of the Lamb, celebrating the readiness of His bride (which is the church of God made up of all believers in Christ here on earth). "Let us rejoice and be glad and give Him glory! For the wedding of the Lamb has come, and His bride has made herself ready." If you are a born-again believer in Christ, you are part of the church, and this qualifies you as being the bride of Christ. Furthermore, Isaiah 54:5 proclaims, "For your Maker is your husband, the LORD Almighty is his name, the Holy One of Israel is your Redeemer; he is called the God of all the earth."

These passages affirm that God has created each person with a designated space in their soul for a spirit spouse. This divine design invites us to choose a connection with Him through Jesus Christ. While not all unbelievers are necessarily bound to an evil spirit spouse, they are particularly vulnerable. The space intended for Jesus can be filled by other spirits, especially when individuals seek solace outside of their relationship with God by committing idolatry usually through sorcery. When this happens, the entity that is introduced is commonly called a "spirit spouse." Based on the explanation above, this entity should be called "an evil spirit spouse." For the sake of simplicity, throughout this book, the evil spirit spouse will be referred to simply as "spirit spouse," but keep in mind that if you have given your life to Jesus Christ, He is your "**Spirit Spouse**." That said, it is important to note that some believers find themselves needing to break free from the grip of an evil spirit spouse that has claimed them, often due to personal or ancestral sin, which is frequently rooted in idolatry.

A Deeper Look at Idolatry

Many people equate idolatry with physical idols like statues or graven images, but idolatry extends far beyond that. Idolatry happens whenever we place something in God's role in our lives.

The Idol That Provokes Lust

Those who experience spirit spouses through constant sexual dreams at night that leave them waking up feeling violated often wonder why it's happening when they're not actively engaging in sexual sin. I remember feeling so confused about this myself. You see my husband is the only man I have ever known sexually, so I couldn't understand why I was being visited in my dreams. I wasn't watching pornography, and I wasn't masturbating, yet something unclean was coming into my sleep and violating me spiritually. That's when the Holy Spirit began to show me that the root of the attack wasn't necessarily sexual. He showed me that, idolatry opens the gate. Consider this powerful passage in Ezekiel 8:5–6:

"Then he said to me, 'Son of man, look toward the north.' So I looked, and in the entrance north of the gate of the altar I saw this idol of jealousy. And he said to me, 'Son of man, do you see what they are doing, the utterly detestable things the Israelites are doing here things that will drive me far from my sanctuary."

God called it *the idol of jealousy*. Some translations call it *the idol that provokes to lust.*

This idol was not placed in the outer courts, but right at the entrance to the altar, polluting the most sacred space. This is exactly how idolatry works in the spirit realm. It doesn't have to look sexual on the outside, but it always draws lust, defilement, and spiritual mixture into God's temple which is *your body* (1 Corinthians 6:19).

In the ancient world, idolatry and sex were almost always tied together. At pagan temples like those for Baal or Asherah; shrine prostitution was part of worship. Both male and female prostitutes served as "priests" and "priestesses," and sexual acts were seen as spiritual transactions to gain favor from the gods. Consider the story of Tamar in Genesis 38. After being mistreated and left childless by Judah's sons, Tamar disguises herself as a shrine prostitute, because she knew that in that culture, sexual practices were deeply tied to idolatry and temple worship. When Judah saw her, he didn't recognize her as his daughter-in-law; he saw what looked like a sacred prostitute and immediately approached her for sex. This wasn't just about lust, it reveals how normalized and spiritualized sex was in pagan worship. To sleep with a prostitute near a shrine was to engage in false worship.

Even though Tamar's motives were different, the context shows us that sex and idolatry were inseparable in the ancient world and that same spirit still operates today, though it's often hidden in modern forms. Here is the truth, even today, any idol you entertain becomes a spiritual shrine, and your soul becomes the temple. You may not lay on a physical altar with a Baal priest, but spiritually, when you trust in money, pride, control, or unhealed wounds more than God, you create a shrine. And when that shrine exists, spirit spouses can come in.

Non-Sexual Idols Can Invite Sexual Spirits

You may not be watching pornography. You may not be masturbating. But idolatry has many disguises. It can look like:

- Love of money or material things.
- Deep pride, self-focus, or unforgiveness.
- Obsession with beauty, image, or influence.
- Soul ties from past relationships.
- Ancestral pacts with false gods or witchcraft.
- Emotional walls built to protect yourself from further pain.
- Trauma that was never surrendered to God.

These things may seem unrelated to sex; but spiritually, they become legal ground for lust and defilement. Just like the idol in Ezekiel's vision, they stand at the doorway of your temple. As Colossians 3:5 says, "Put to death, therefore, whatever belongs to your earthly nature: sexual immorality, impurity, lust, evil desires and greed, which is idolatry. "That last line says it plainly; *Greed is idolatry too*. All of it is part of the same polluted altar.

Unhealed Wounds Can Become Soul Shrines

To truly begin the journey of deliverance, we must reflect on our life's story and identify when we experienced any form of trauma that deeply wounded us. Often, demons live in these unhealed wounds, waiting for the right opportunity to take hold. It is important to note that when wounds are not taken to God for healing, they can get passed down from one generation to another. These unhealed wounds cause us to build conscious or unconscious walls to protect ourselves from being hurt again. The problem is that the walls we build can become idols, thus becoming a gateway to spirit spouse attachments. We are not meant to rely on ourselves for protection. When we create systems to defend ourselves instead of relying on God, we unknowingly commit idolatry. The walls we create in response to pain often act as barriers to experiencing God's love in its fullness.

Some Common Symptoms Accompanying a Spirit Spouse

1. **Disturbing Sexual Dreams:** These may manifest as sexual encounters with inappropriate figures, such as family members, including children, spiritual leaders,

or even same-sex partners. Such dreams often indicate a spirit spouse's influence, which aims to confuse and destabilize the individual's sexual and emotional boundaries.

2. **Watching Others Have Sex:** Dreams where you observe others engaging in sexual acts, often with a pornographic undertone, can signify a voyeuristic spirit at work. This symptom reflects the tormenting nature of a spirit spouse, who uses these dreams to instill shame and confusion.

3. **Dreams of Eating:** The Bible highlights the significance of eating in establishing spiritual covenants. In 1 Corinthians 11:26, taking communion symbolizes our declaration of Christ's sacrifice and the new covenant. When afflicted by a spirit spouse, recurrent dreams of eating can signify participation in a demonic covenant. These dreams often involve consuming strange foods, which mimic the act of communion but pervert the true intention of spiritual nourishment, reinforcing ties to evil spirits.

4. **Sleep Paralysis:** Individuals may experience an overwhelming sensation of being pinned down during sleep, often accompanied by a feeling of a malevolent

presence. This symptom frequently points to spiritual oppression by a spirit spouse.

5. **Strange Physical Sensations:** Many report feelings of something crawling within their body or sensations akin to a baby moving in their womb. These experiences are indicative of the invasive nature of a spirit spouse, seeking to assert control over the individual's physical and emotional state.

6. **Recurring Dreams of Dead People:** Visions of deceased individuals can signal unresolved issues, necromancy, or an unhealthy fixation on the past, often indicating that a spirit spouse is drawing on these emotional ties to exert influence.

7. **Marital and Relational Problems:** Persistent issues in family or romantic relationships, characterized by emotional disunity or difficulties in commitment, narcissistic-based relationships, etc., can be traced back to the interference of spirit spouses, complicating the dynamics of love and intimacy.

8. **Inability to Use Gifts and Talents:** An unexplained blockage or inability to express personal abilities and talents can signify a spirit spouse's attempt to hinder personal growth and fulfillment, often leading to feelings of frustration and stagnation.

9. **Strange Infirmities:** Physical ailments that lack a clear medical cause and/or recurrent pattern, like infirmities, can be symptomatic of spiritual issues and often linked to the influence of a spirit spouse.

10. **Severe Financial Hardship:** Persistent financial struggles, despite hard work and planning, with no logical explanation.

11. **Mental Illness:** Strange or irrational fears (e.g., fear of swallowing food), panic attacks, anxiety, or bipolar disorder, which may sometimes have spiritual origins.

12. **Sexual Immorality:** Uncontrolled urges, perversion, same-sex attraction, or habitual uncontrollable sexual sin.

13. **Emotional Frigidity:** Difficulty forming or maintaining emotional connections or experiencing emotional detachment.

14. **Sexual Issues:** Problems in marital intimacy, unexplainable aversion to a spouse, sexual frigidity, or hypersexual tendencies.

15. **Strange Infirmities Related to Reproduction:** Conditions such as recurrent pregnancy loss or infertility with or without medical explanation, low sperm count, and barrenness.

16. **Closed Gate Syndrome:** Unexplained blockages in progress, repeated failure or stagnation in personal, professional, or spiritual growth despite consistent effort.

Some Common Gateways to the Spirit Spouse Covenant

The Practice of Witchcraft

The practice of witchcraft, whether through rituals, spells, divination, or even seemingly "harmless" forms like horoscopes or ancestral worship, naming ceremonies, the crowning of chiefs, etc., serves as a spiritual gateway that invites demonic attachments, including spirit spouses. These entities gain legal access through the violation of God's commandments and the seeking of power or knowledge apart from Him (Deuteronomy 18:10-12).

Where I come from, one example vividly comes to mind. When a baby is born with dreaded hair, hair that naturally forms in twists or knots. This is often seen as a spiritual mark, a sign that the child holds some unique connection to the unseen world. In many communities, such children are thought to carry a special purpose or blessing. As a result, tradition dictates that this child be taken to a shrine, where they undergo specific rituals, prayers, and offerings dedicated to deities or spirits by a spiritual guide or priest. To an outsider, these rites might seem like an innocent part of family heritage, an act of reverence toward ancestors. Yet behind this practice lies a dangerous, often hidden reality. Such rituals, though culturally normalized, establish spiritual covenants that can open doors to spirit spouses and other forms of demonic bondage.

Spirit spouses often enter through these covenants, whether made knowingly or unknowingly, and torment individuals emotionally, mentally, sexually, and relationally. What begins as a search for identity, protection, or healing through witchcraft becomes a cycle of bondage, as these spirits demand loyalty and actively disrupt God's original design for intimacy and covenant. True freedom begins when these practices are renounced, and the heart is fully submitted to the Lordship of Jesus Christ. God warns clearly in His Word: "Should not a people inquire of their God? Why consult the dead on behalf of the living?" (Isaiah 8:19).

Modern Idolatry

In our modern world, ancient rites and ancestral curses may appear hidden, yet they're alive and well wrapped in "entertainment," "self-discovery," or "enlightenment." The pathways that once led to ancestral shrines have re-emerged in new forms, adapting to the language and technology of today's society. What once required a visit to a secluded shrine can now be accessed with a few taps on a smartphone, and what once involved ceremonies deep in the forest now unfolds openly on social media feeds.

People often turn to tarot cards, horoscopes, psychic readings, and other occult practices out of curiosity, self-exploration, or seeking answers about the future. Platforms like Instagram, TikTok, and YouTube are filled with influencers and practitioners who use polished aesthetics to promote satanic spiritual services, personalized tarot readings, star sign analyses, and even "spirit guides" who supposedly help connect people to hidden knowledge. These practices are presented as harmless, trendy, and intriguing, but beneath this modern gloss lies an ancient trap. Each interaction, consultation, or reading is, in reality, a spiritual contract. It opens a door, creating a legal right for spirits to enter and influence one's life, relationships, and destiny.

Take **horoscopes**, for example. Scrolling through a daily astrology post may seem like an innocent way to pass time or even as a fun way to gain "insight" into one's day. But in the spiritual realm, this seemingly trivial engagement with astrology can act as a spiritual invitation. Each time someone aligns themselves with a horoscope, believing it has power over their life, they unknowingly grant spirits a level of control over their decisions, emotions, and relationships. These horoscopes function as a subtle gateway, allowing entities access to shape a person's identity, guiding their actions according to a script that does not come from God.

Let us recall what the Lord tells us in Deuteronomy 18:10 (AMP). "There shall not be found among you anyone who makes his son or daughter pass through the fire [as a sacrifice], one who uses divination and fortune-telling, one who practices witchcraft, or one who interprets omens, or a sorcerer. "Even childlike games, like using a Ouija board, dabbling in necromancy, or attempting to summon spirits, are powerful rituals in disguise. Social media platforms have made it easy to encounter such practices, often wrapped in "spooky fun" around certain times of the year. Yet, these interactions are not mere games. By engaging with such practices, individuals create lasting bonds with the very spirits that lurk behind them. In return for a moment of thrill, they may experience spiritual oppression, a sense of being watched, or a dark presence following them. Modern idolatry is also woven into "manifestation" practices, where people are encouraged to "speak things into existence" using affirmations and energy manipulation. While there is power in words, aligning oneself with spiritual forces outside of God creates a direct channel for demonic influence. In some cases, manifestation is associated with consulting "spirit guides" or "ascended masters" for help in shaping one's future. Yet, these spirits, no matter how benevolent they appear, are not from God. They eagerly use these practices to claim authority over a person's life, drawing them further into bondage.

Video games, too, can be an open door. Many popular games immerse players in supernatural worlds where summoning spirits, performing dark rituals, or wielding otherworldly powers are part of the experience. These interactions, while virtual, mirror real spiritual practices, inviting players to engage with forces they may not fully understand. Without realizing it, they open themselves to influences that can cause confusion, nightmares, and inner chaos. And for some, these games are just the beginning, a gateway that sparks curiosity and leads them deeper into the occult.

Movies steeped in horror or occult themes take this influence further. The disturbing images, dark rituals, and demonic characters linger in viewers' minds long after the screen goes off. These visuals are not just fiction; they are a portal to evil spirits. Spirit spouses are quick to seize on these open doors, using these dreams and mental impressions as entry points to entangle their victims in bondage.

Those who would be candidates for spirit spouses only due to ancestral pacts may now face the same bondage through modern idolatry. Whether masked as a "fun" horoscope, "helpful" psychic reading, or fear-based entertainment, these practices lure people into covenants with powers they cannot see, enslaving them as surely as the ancient altars once did. But the answer, now as ever, lies in Jesus, the one who breaks every chain, nullifying every hidden agreement and restoring freedom to those who seek Him. It is important to note here that if an individual is born with an inherited spirit spouse, they will feel drawn to the practices described above.

Halloween: Witches and Ghosts

Halloween, as we know it today, has evolved from ancient Celtic celebrations, particularly the festival of Samhain. Samhain marked the end of harvest and the start of winter, a time when the Celts believed the boundary between the living and the dead became thin, allowing spirits to wander freely. People would leave offerings and light bonfires to appease these spirits, hoping to avoid misfortune. Later, Halloween was merged with Christian practices to become "All Hallows' Eve," a time meant to honor the saints. Yet, it retained many of the eerie and supernatural elements of Samhain, evolving into a night where spiritual forces and the themes of death, mystery, and even witchcraft are woven into the fabric of Halloween traditions.

As Christianity spread, it redefined or replaced many pagan festivals with Christian observances. However, certain Halloween traditions, like costumes representing witches and ghosts, kept elements of Samhain alive. Costumes, ghost stories, and practices connected to the occult became standard.

Why Should Christians Care?

Many Christians view Halloween as harmless fun, but this mindset can dull our spiritual discernment. Symbols of witchcraft, ghosts, and the occult are not just fantasy; they represent real spiritual forces. Celebrating them, even playfully, can open doors to darkness that aren't easily closed. The Bible warns us, "Have nothing to do with the fruitless deeds of darkness but rather expose them" (Ephesians 5:11). This isn't outdated advice. It is a clear call to stay spiritually alert. In cultures where witchcraft is openly practiced, people know these forces aren't harmless. Yet in the West, dismissing the spiritual realm as fiction is easy, leaving us vulnerable to deception.

1 Peter 5:8 urges us to be sober-minded and watchful because the enemy always seeks to devour. Halloween's themes of death and darkness may seem like innocent fun, but they can desensitize us and dull our spiritual sensitivity over time. Even more concerning is how Halloween is becoming accepted in Christian circles, leading to confusion and compromise. We must be wise and discerning about what we engage with. What we treat lightly may carry serious spiritual consequences for us and those watching us.

My Story

Let me share the experience we had when we visited a pumpkin patch in California, USA, during Halloween. The decorations honored the season: bouncy jumpers for kids, pumpkins, eerie ghost figures, and cobwebs hanging from the trees. At first glance, it all seemed like harmless fun, just another Halloween celebration filled with costumes and laughter. We didn't think much of it as the kids ran around with their friends, and the adults chatted and enjoyed the evening. But that night, as we returned home, something strange began to happen. Our children, who had been full of energy and excitement just hours earlier, suddenly became restless. They couldn't settle down or relax. They tossed and turned in bed, clearly disturbed by something they couldn't put into words.

The night dragged on, and it became clear that they were not going to sleep. My husband and I tried to comfort them, but nothing seemed to help. The fear that gripped them was palpable.

As the hours passed, it was no longer just a typical case of being scared after a spooky night. This was different. It felt as though the fear had attached itself to them, lingering in the air. Our children were not able to find peace, and it was clear that something was spiritually off. At that moment, my husband and I both realized that the environment we had been in that evening might have opened the door to something darker. What we thought was innocent fun had somehow invited the spirit of fear into our home.

We gathered our children and began to pray and anoint them with oil. We repented and asked God to forgive us for opening the door to evil in our home. We commanded the spirit of fear that had gripped their hearts to leave in Jesus' name. We asked God to protect our home and to restore His peace in their spirits. As we prayed, we felt a noticeable shift in the atmosphere. It was as if the heaviness that had settled on us started to lift, and the peace of God flooded the room. Slowly but surely, the tension began to ease, and our children, who had been wide-eyed and frightened, started to relax. Eventually, they were able to fall asleep.

That night, we learned a powerful lesson. We realized that the spiritual atmosphere surrounding the pumpkin patch celebrating Halloween (which we had walked into thinking it was a harmless, fun celebration) had actually opened the door to a spirit of fear. Even something as seemingly innocent as Halloween decorations had invited an unsettling spiritual influence into our home. It wasn't just a case of bad dreams; it was a spiritual attack on our peace.

Practical Steps to Break Witchcraft Pacts

1. Repent and Renounce All Involvement in Witchcraft: The first step in deliverance is repentance. We must take responsibility, not just for our own sins but for the sins of our ancestors if necessary (Numbers 14:18). Here is a prayer to begin the process: "Lord Jesus, today I repent of the sin of idolatry practiced by my ancestors and myself. I ask you to forgive me and my generational line for making covenants with demons through the worship of graven images. Please forgive me for depending on evil spirits and for seeking guidance from witch doctors, tarot readers, and other oc-

cult practices. I renounce this sin and ask that you reveal any hidden idolatry within me, whether it be self-dependence, reliance on others, or people-pleasing. Please forgive me and cleanse my bloodline according to Your Word in 1 John 1:9. In Jesus' name, amen."

2. Destroy All Occult Items: Physically remove and destroy any objects tied to witchcraft (books, jewelry, charms, and idols). "A number who had practiced sorcery brought their scrolls together and burned them publicly" (Acts 19:19). Don't give them away; destroy them.

3. Invite the Holy Spirit to Fill Every Area That Was Occupied: After deliverance, spiritual housecleaning must be followed by Holy Spirit infilling. "When an impure spirit comes out of a person... When it arrives, it finds the house unoccupied, swept clean and put in order then it goes and takes with it seven other spirits more wicked than itself, and they go in and live there. And the final condition of that person is worse than the first." (Matthew 12:43–45). Ask God to fill your heart, mind, and body with His presence and truth.

4. Engage in Ongoing Spiritual Warfare and Healing: Use the Word of God, worship, and prayer to maintain freedom and protect yourself from re-infestation.

"Submit yourselves, then, to God. Resist the devil, and he will flee from you" (James 4:7). Regularly fast, pray, and declare your identity in Christ.

5. Stay Accountable and Seek Discipleship: Surround yourself with godly mentors and a Bible-believing community for accountability and growth. "Confess your sins to each other and pray for each other so that you may be healed" (James 5:16).

6. Pursue Inner Healing and Address Soul Ties: Identify and break emotional or sexual soul ties that may keep the demonic covenant alive. "What harmony is there between Christ and Belial? Come out from them and be separate" (2 Corinthians 6:14–17).

Who is the Spirit Spouse in Your life? Uprooting the Strong Man

Maybe you picked up this book because you're locked in a spiritual battle with a spirit spouse but nothing you've tried has brought lasting freedom. You may have read the previous chapters on witchcraft and thought, "But I've never practiced witchcraft. I've never visited a witch doctor or knowingly made a pact with darkness." And yet, you still feel tormented in your dreams, blocked in relationships, or spiritually bound in your soul. If that's you, I want to offer something deeper than a surface-level explanation. What you're dealing with is not "just a demon." It is a spiritual entity that reflects a particular identity, character trait, or emotional stronghold that was either passed down, invited through trauma, or through agreement.

This is not just about what you've done. It's about what has been spoken over you, what has been modeled before you, and what you may have absorbed without knowing. In the next few paragraphs, I want to help you go beyond casting out symptoms and start identifying what is behind the pattern because once you see it, you can name it, confront it, and overthrow it. Let's begin by exploring a key biblical principle which is **the strongman**. But before we dive in, I want to ask you two questions, these two questions changed everything for me. They are questions which I heard God ask me clearly during my time of prayer and I believe they're going to mark a turning point for you too.

What is the name of the spirit spouse you are dealing with? Where does it live?

These questions are not just symbolic; they are strategic. They expose the strongman. According to Mark 3:27, "No one can enter a strong man's house without first tying him up. Then he can plunder the strong man's house." This verse reveals a powerful truth. The strongman is a real demonic force. He is a spiritual entity that gains legal access to your life through generational sin, trauma, or personal choices. He builds spiritual strongholds in your soul by working through sin patterns like anger, fear, lust, pride, or control. These patterns often produce destructive pain patterns, poverty, addiction, sickness, and depression that feel impossible to escape. **The name of the strongman is the identity of the spirit spouse you are dealing with.**

The strongman takes up residence in your **character and habits**, shaping behaviors and mindsets that keep you bound. But once you **identify him**, you can tie him up and take back what he's stolen. This strongman is often tied to ancestral covenants, agreements your forefathers made with demonic forces (through witchcraft, as discussed above) to escape pain. These agreements open the door to spirit spouses, demonic entities that attack through dreams and influence your thoughts, habits, and relationships. Think of it like a tree: Hebrews 12:15, "See to it... that no bitter root grows up to cause trouble and defile many."

Roots = sin and wounds (rejection, pride, fear, etc.).

Trunk = generational curses or ancestral spirits.

Fruit = the visible struggles in your life (poverty, broken relationships, illness).

Deliverance isn't just about saying prayers or commanding demons to leave. You must identify how these spiritual patterns show up in your character, repent, and allow God to transform those areas. True freedom comes from applying God's truth, love, joy, worship, grace, warfare, faith, and freedom and walking in new habits. Ultimately, defeating the strongman means confronting your sin patterns and wounds, recognizing the generational roots, and replacing them with God's truth.

How to Defeat the Strongman

1. Identify the root wound and sin pattern.
2. Repent and renounce the agreement.
3. Apply the Word and walk in new habits.
4. Pray with revelation, not just repetition.
5. Use the 7 keys: love, joy, worship, grace, warfare, faith, and freedom to deal with the unique recurring pain pattern you identify in your life.

Breaking Generational Strongholds Requires Testing and Transformation

To be free from the generational strongman, God will test you in the very areas where your ancestors fell, not to punish you but to give you the chance to respond differently by using godly coping skills rooted in the Word:

1. **Love** (1 John 4:18)

2. **Joy** (Nehemiah 8:10)

3. **Worship** (John 4:24)

4. **Grace** (2 Corinthians 12:9)

5. **Warfare** (Ephesians 6:12)

6. **Faith** (Hebrews 11:6)

7. **Freedom** (Galatians 5:1)

"Then Jesus said to His disciples, 'Whoever wants to be my disciple must deny themselves and take up their cross and follow me'" (Matthew 16:24).

Testing by Fire: The Example of Poverty

If poverty was the pain pattern in your bloodline that led your ancestors to look for help outside of God, you might enter a season of lack even while praying and fasting, not because

God has abandoned you, but because He is refining you. 1 Peter 1:7, "These trials will show that your faith is genuine... tested as fire tests and purifies gold." You must reject generational behaviors (complaining, borrowing without repaying, stinginess, image-driven spending) and instead:

- ❖ Seek wisdom from the Holy Spirit.
- ❖ Take practical steps (e.g., financial classes, responsible stewardship).
- ❖ Leave behind destructive relationships and habits.

The pain pattern (e.g. poverty, rejection, addiction) is not the real enemy; it's a symptom of a deeper root sin pattern (e.g., pride, fear, disobedience). Until you deal with the sin, the pain will return. Romans 6:12, "Therefore do not let sin reign in your mortal body so that you obey its evil desires." Deliverance is not about using God to stop the pain; it's about surrendering to Him so He can heal the root. Otherwise, you're still trying to fix a spiritual issue with human solutions.

Misplaced Motives Block Deliverance

When your motive is just to end the suffering, you're still operating like your ancestors, who practiced witchcraft, seeking freedom apart from intimacy with Jesus. But when your desperation becomes to end the sin pattern, to walk closely with Christ, you are truly ready. John 15:5-8, "If you remain in me and I in you, you will bear much fruit... This is to my Father's glory, that you bear much fruit..."

Deliverance = Authority Rooted in Intimacy

You cannot command the strongman to leave if you keep entertaining him. True authority in the spirit realm comes when you:

- ❖ Obey God in secret
- ❖ Embrace holiness
- ❖ Desire transformation more than relief

2 Corinthians 10:6, "And we will be ready to punish every act of disobedience, once your obedience is complete." You become the curse-breaker not just by praying hard but by living holy. When your heart burns more for Christ than comfort, you become the one the strongman must obey.

1. **Tests will come** where past generations failed, so pass them God's way.
2. **Write down** old patterns and renounce them; choose godly alternatives.
3. **Shift your focus** from ending pain to ending sin.
4. **Deliverance is a journey of intimacy**, not just escape.
5. **Fruit-bearing through abiding in Christ** is the true sign of freedom.

Prayer to Identify the Strongman and Repent of Sin Patterns

Heavenly Father, please reveal to me what specific spirit is the generational ancestral strongman operating in my life. (You can take a fast for this if it is not immediately clear to you.)

Heavenly Father, I stand on behalf of myself, all past generations, and future generations, and I repent for the fact that we have entertained and obeyed [insert the name of the strongman spirit God has shown you here, e.g., fear, lust, witchcraft, discord, etc.].

Please give me the power through Your Holy Spirit to disobey the generational ancestral instructions of the ancestral strongman in my family line. (Call out the strongman here (fear, lust, etc.)

Heavenly Father, by my will and with Your power, I declare and decree that I am no longer controlled by the sin patterns of the generational strongman (fear, lust, gossip, etc.) that have existed in my family line.

Please, Heavenly Father, shine your light of deliverance into me and show me how I am obeying the strongman (spirit of fear, spirit of lust, etc.) in my character and habits.

I become stronger than the strongman (insert strongman here) today by the power of the Holy Spirit.

Please, Lord, open my ears to hear and discern generational instructional whispers of the strongman so I can disobey them and shut them off in Jesus' name.

I shut off all generational instructional whispers of the strongman from my children and future generations. I terminate your assignment in their lives in the mighty name of Jesus.

You, generational strongman of ___, terminate your assignment in my life NOW and forever in Jesus' name.

Pray for your spouse if you are married and your spouse is not praying these prayers with you.

Heavenly Father, help me to have a renewed appetite for Your Word so that my brain can be rewired to not function based on the remote-control generational strongman of ___(say the name of the strongman God has revealed to you) instructions.

I disconnect my life and destiny and that of my children from the remote-control power of the generational strongman in Jesus' name.

I declare Romans 8:2 over myself and all future generations: through Christ, the Spirit that gives life has set me free from the spirit of sin and death.

Narcissistic Relationships as Gateways/Manifestations

One of the most destructive expressions of inherited spirit spouses through ancestral pacts manifests through narcissistic relationships, relationships that entangle their victims in a web of manipulation, emotional torment, and control. This isn't just psychological; it's deeply spiritual, rooted in the influence of the Ahab and Jezebel spirits. These spirits operate together, feeding off domination and submission, leaving a trail of shattered confidence, fractured self-worth, and deep confusion.

Narcissism is not a random personality flaw; it is often a generational stronghold passed down through family lines. In homes where manipulation and emotional abuse are normalized, children grow up thinking this dysfunction is love. They become either the dominator or the dominated, continuing the toxic cycle. The Jezebel spirit thrives on control, while the Ahab spirit enables this behavior, sacrificing its own identity in the process. Together, they create a dynamic that is as spiritually oppressive as it is emotionally destructive. These narcissistic spirits usually gain access in families where favoritism is practiced.

Discerning Narcissistic Relationships

Staying in a narcissistic relationship is an open door for the spirit spouse to continue its torment. These relationships often begin like a dream. The narcissist knows how to captivate, to charm, to make their victim feel chosen. But soon, the dream becomes a nightmare. Gas lighting, blame-shifting, and emotional abuse replace the affection, leaving the victim questioning their worth, their sanity, and even their purpose. This mirrors the role of a spirit spouse, which seeks to enslave its host through violation and control.

The Bible is clear in its warnings against such toxicity. In Revelation 2:20, God commands us not to tolerate Jezebel, who seduces and manipulates for power. This isn't just an instruction; it's a lifeline, as this bondage can even lead to premature death. Tolerating these spirits in our relationships allows them to tighten their grip, not only on our emotional state but also on our spiritual freedom. Proverbs 4:23 gives another piece of wisdom, "Above all else, guard your heart, for everything you do flows from it." Guarding your heart means discerning what you allow into your life, especially in the form of relationships.

Breaking free from a narcissistic relationship is not merely about escaping abuse; it's about reclaiming your identity and rejecting the spiritual strongholds that have kept you bound. It is about refusing to give your worship to the person who seeks to dominate you and giving your worship back to the God who created you. Recognizing the signs is the first step. Narcissists thrive on control, wanting to be the god you serve; they leave you emotionally drained, spiritually disconnected, and physically ill. But once you see the pattern, you can begin the process of deliverance. Walking away from a narcissistic relationship can feel terrifying, but it's an act of obedience and faith, a step toward the freedom God has for you.

Negative Soul Ties: A Hidden Chain

Soul ties are created in guilt, fear, and fake love. These invisible cords often stem from ancestral spirit spouse covenants and open the door to controlling spirits like Jezebel (1 Kings 21:25), leading to demonic bondage. They masquerade as love but destroy marriages, families, and generations and are most times at the root of spirit spouse bondages. Consider the following examples:

The Mother-Son Tie

This is a situation we see all too often. A man is married, but emotionally, he's still tied to his mother, not in a healthy, honoring way, but in a way that interferes with his ability to fully connect with his wife. His mother raised him, protected him, and may have even sacrificed a lot for him, but now, she can't let go. That emotional grip creates a soul tie, and without realizing it, she ends up acting like a gatekeeper in his marriage. The Bible makes it clear in Genesis 2:24 that "a man leaves his father and mother and is united to his wife, and they become one flesh." That "leaving" doesn't mean abandoning your parents, but it does mean shifting loyalty and priority. When that shift doesn't happen, it creates confusion and conflict.

So even though he's legally a husband, he's still emotionally a son who feels trapped. Guilt and fear prevent him from setting healthy boundaries with his mom. As a result, his wife starts to feel like a stranger in her own home, fighting an invisible force. Spiritually, it's as if his mother's presence keeps whispering, "Your wife isn't enough." The Bible says, "Honor your father and your mother" (Exodus 20:12), but honor doesn't mean unlimited obedience, especially when their influence goes against God's design for marriage. Exodus 20:3 reminds us, "You shall have no other gods before me." That includes placing someone else's voice, even a parent's, above God's Word. When a soul tie like this is in place, it weakens the man's spiritual leadership and opens the door to strife in the home.

The Mother-Daughter Tie

Just like some men struggle to fully become husbands because they're still tied to their mothers, the same thing happens with women. A woman can be married yet emotionally still attached to her mother in a way that affects her marriage. Maybe her mom was her best friend, her safe place growing up. She raised her, comforted her, but never released her. Now the daughter is married, but she's still carrying her mother's opinions into every decision. She wants to please her husband, but she's still looking over her shoulder, wondering, what will my mom think? Meanwhile, the mother may feel left out, replaced, or even jealous. So, she begins to speak little things that plant doubt:

"Are you sure he really loves you?"

"He's not from our tribe, how will that work?"

"He's not what I had in mind for you."

These comments seem small, but they carry weight. The daughter, trying to stay loyal to both, becomes torn. She's a wife on paper but a daughter in bondage. Her husband begins to feel like he's competing with someone he never signed up to fight: his mother-in-law's spiritual influence. This is what we call spiritual adultery because, emotionally and spiritually, she's divided. Jesus said in Matthew 6:24, "No one can serve two masters." In marriage, there can't be split allegiance. Once you're joined to your spouse that becomes your first human covenant. You can still honor your parents, but your loyalty shifts.

In some cases, it even gets darker. Some mothers speak curses without even realizing the spiritual damage they're causing. Some may turn to cultural rituals or even witchcraft to "protect" or "control" their child's marriage. This opens a door for strife, confusion, and sometimes even premature death. So, just like a man must break unhealthy soul ties with his mother to become the head of his home, a woman must do the same to become a fully present, spiritually aligned wife. Marriage requires leaving and cleaving not just physically, but emotionally and spiritually too.

Friends & Family: The Outer Circle of Control

Soul ties aren't limited to parents. They can extend to friends, pastors, siblings, and even objects or animals. They can be anything that takes God's place in your heart (Deuteronomy 5:7). The spirit of Jezebel, the spirit of control, which is a spirit of witchcraft, recruits anyone willing to guilt, manipulate, or override your boundaries.

It can be manifested by the friend who says, "You've changed," when you protect your marriage. The sibling who

49

guilt's you. The relative who mocks your boundaries. Then there is the Ahab spirit, which whispers to you, "They're all you've got." So, you bend and you compromise. Without realizing it, you renew your covenant with the very spirit spouse you are trying to break from because of what you may consider family loyalty. Jesus reminds us through His Word that, "If anyone comes to me and does not hate father and mother, wife and children, brothers and sisters, yes, even their own life, such a person cannot be my disciple" (Luke 14:26).

HOW TO BREAK FREE

The controlling spirit is at its core the spirit of witchcraft, and it is a liar. It says the soul tie is unbreakable. It says freedom will cost too much. It says you're too weak. But Jesus says, "If the Son sets you free, you will be free indeed" (John 8:36). He broke every chain on the cross, and His power lives in you. This is a spiritual war, but you're not alone. The controlling spirit is no match for the Holy Spirit. The soul tie is no match for God's truth. Freedom is yours, but it requires action, courage, and faith.

For the son or daughter

Name the soul tie. Call it out, mother-son, mother-daughter, friend, family. Bring it into the light where the enemy can't hide. "The light shines in the darkness, and the darkness has not overcome it" (John 1:5).

Repent

God has watched this demonic pattern play out generation after generation. It has stopped Him from doing what He wants to do with your family. It has wounded His heart more than it has destroyed your family. Yahweh hurts! He is looking for someone who will be courageous enough to stop the mess. He hurts! Take time out to repent on behalf of yourself and all past generations for this sin of forming demonic soul ties.

Break the vows. Renounce them in Jesus' name. Pray, "Lord, I break every vow that ties me to my mother, father, friend, or family. Set me free by your blood in Jesus' name."

Set boundaries. Honor your parents, but don't worship them. Remember, honor can look like distance; distance is better than being triggered into disrespect. Love your friends, but don't worship them. Say, "I value your opinion, but this is my home, my life, my choice." Stand firm, even if they push back.

Pray in power. In upcoming chapters, we will share how praying in tongues builds your spiritual strength. If you have been blessed with this gift, use it to confuse the controlling spirit and align with God's authority. Pray for clarity, courage, and freedom.

Choose your covenant. If married, make your spouse your priority. Tell your mother-in-law, "My wife and I are the decision makers in our home." If single, chase God's purpose, not your mother's approval.

Forgive and heal. The controlling spirit feeds on your wounds. Guilt, fear, rejection. Forgive your parents, friends, or family for their control. Ask God to heal the pain that keeps you bound.

For the spouse

Fight for your marriage. Your spouse isn't the enemy; the controlling spirit is. Pray for their freedom. Ask God to break the soul tie binding them to their mother, family or friends.

Claim your place. You're not an outsider; you're God's chosen partner. Tell your mother-in-law, "This is our home, and we make the decisions." Speak with love but stand with strength.

Break the spiritual attack. Bind the controlling spirit in Jesus' name. Pray, "I loose God's peace, unity, and love over this home" (Matthew 18:18). I command a divorce between the spiritual spouses married to my spouse through his mother in Jesus' name.

Dreams of Eating a Manifestation of Witchcraft Covenants

The presence of a spirit spouse in one's life is often marked by continuous disturbing dreams of eating. Eating in dreams is a particularly deceptive and dangerous tactic. It mirrors the holy act of communion, twisting it into a perverted ritual that binds individuals to demonic agreements and is often followed by seasons of strange infirmities. Dreams of eating when one is battling a spirit spouse are not mere figments of the imagination; they are important spiritual markers, often pointing to the existence of unseen agreements and covenants at work.

When Jesus gathered His disciples for the Last Supper, He used the act of eating to signify the most sacred of covenants. He said, "This is my body, given for you; do this in remembrance of me. This cup is the new covenant in my blood, which is poured out for you" (Luke 22:19–20). By instructing His followers to partake of the bread and wine, He established a powerful declaration: eating was an act of affirming their relationship with Him, rooted in the sacrifice He was about to make. Every time believers take communion, they proclaim

His death and victory over sin and darkness, as stated in 1 Corinthians 11:26.

But just as God uses this act to draw us closer to Him, Satan seeks to mimic and distort its meaning, using eating as a tool for spiritual bondage. In the spiritual realm, eating can symbolize agreement, participation, and allegiance. To eat at the Lord's Table is to affirm one's covenant with Christ, but to partake in what belongs to idols is to declare allegiance to demonic powers, Acts 15:28). In the same way, dreams of eating can serve as a spiritual transaction, a declaration of covenants with forces that oppose God's will.

Consistent dreams of eating, therefore, must not be dismissed or taken lightly. They are an invitation to look deeper, to seek God's wisdom, and to walk in the freedom that comes from living in covenant with Him alone. As I cried out to God for deliverance, he began to open my eyes to the fact that, after I allowed myself to participate in the sins we will explore below, I would experience dreams of eating strange foods, followed by tormenting encounters with a spirit spouse which led to seasons of severe infirmity. Among these, sins of the mouth are particularly significant. The mouth, a powerful tool for life and blessing, can also become a gateway to bondage when misused. Let's explore how specific mouth sins serve as open gates:

Gossip: The Sweet Poison

Proverbs 18:8 paints a profound picture of gossip, likening it to "choice morsels" that slip deep into the inner most parts of a person. At first glance, gossip may seem harmless, a fleeting exchange of words or a casual comment shared between friends. But these "morsels," sweet as they may appear, carry within them a poison that can corrupt relationships. In a world where communication flows freely, gossip often emerges as one of the most subtle yet common forms of spoken sin.

The act of gossip reflects a deep, underlying insecurity and a lack of self-control. When we gossip, we often seek to validate ourselves by belittling others and to feel significant by tearing others down. It's a reflection of our own fears of inadequacy, of being unnoticed, of not measuring up. When you find yourself constantly gossiping with someone, this is an indication that you do not have a true relationship with them. Gossip becomes a way to gain attention and feel significant, but in reality, it only exposes our vulnerability. It reveals a heart that is not secure in its worth or its place in the world. When we speak negatively of others, we often project our own pain, unhealed wounds, and our need for validation onto those around us. It's a cry for significance, a desperate attempt to feel seen or heard, but it comes at the expense of someone else's reputation or peace.

But as Proverbs 18:8 warns, gossip is never just a harmless exchange of words. It is a choice morsel, which goes down to the soul. This verse supports the fact that gossip is spiritual food and if it is already a morsel within a person's soul then it can show up within the dream as food being eaten. When gossip takes root, it creates walls between individuals, cutting them off from understanding and intimacy. The spirit spouse uses these walls to isolate people, feeding on their loneliness and confusion.

We must remember that in the spirit realm our mouths are like cups that God wants to use to pour fresh water onto people to bless them. When we yield to gossip, our mouths become dirty cups, and God is unable to use us to bless others. But there is hope. As Christians, we can talk to God about what we feel the need to gossip about. We can bring the people that we are tempted to gossip about before God and pray for them. When we do this, we will rid ourselves of the desire to engage in gossip or listen to gossip.

Complaining: A Voice of Ingratitude

The Bible provides numerous examples of how complaining leads to spiritual defeat. One of the most striking examples is found in the story of the Israelites in the wilderness. After being delivered from centuries of slavery in Egypt and witnessing the miraculous parting of the Red Sea, they were given every reason to trust God. Yet, time and again, they murmured against Him. Despite His faithful provision of manna from Heaven, water from a rock, and protection from enemies, they constantly grumbled. Their complaints were not just about their circumstances but reflected a deeper dissatisfaction with God Himself.

One of the ways the spirit spouse operated in my life was through complaining. I didn't realize it at first, but every time I complained about something, my singleness, my health, my lack, I'd find myself in a worse situation. Life would fold in such a way that I'd start wishing for the very thing I was once complaining about because my complaining had brought on an even more difficult season of the very thing I was complaining about. God delivered me from this when He opened by eyes to see that seasons of complaining gave birth to seasons of dream eating which gave birth to spirit spouse sexual encounters and then ended in seasons of unexplained infirmity. This cycle is not just emotional, it is spiritual. It's one of the ways the enemy keeps you bound and blind. Complaining isn't harmless. It opens doors. Numbers 21:4–6 "But the people grew impatient on the way; they spoke against God and against Moses, and said, 'Why have you brought us up out of Egypt to die in the wilderness? There is no bread! There is no water! And we detest this miserable food!' Then the Lord sent venomous snakes among them; they bit the people, and many Israelites died."

This pattern of complaining isn't limited to the Old Testament. Even the Apostle Paul, in Philippians 2:14-15, warns believers, "Do everything without grumbling or arguing, so that you may become blameless and pure, "children of God without fault in a warped and crooked generation." Then you will shine among them like stars in the sky." Complaining can tarnish our testimony as believers. It damages our ability to witness to those around us. Our lives are meant to reflect the light of Christ, but a heart of complaining hides that light, making us indistinguishable from the very world we are called to illuminate.

Complaining opens the door to a spirit of discontentment and rebellion. It's a subtle invitation for the enemy to sow seeds of negativity and dissatisfaction. In Romans 1:21, Paul speaks of the downward spiral that begins with a failure to recognize God's goodness, "For although they knew God, they neither glorified him as God nor gave thanks to him, but their thinking became futile, and their foolish hearts were darkened."

The Trap of Fear

Self-Preservation

Fear often masquerades as self-protection, convincing us that hiding is wise. We tell ourselves that by staying in the shadows, we're avoiding rejection, criticism, or envy. But this self-preservation is a subtle form of idolatry. It places more trust in our ability to control outcomes than in God's power to protect and elevate us. When Jesus said, "Let your light shine before others" (Matthew 5:16), He wasn't merely giving a suggestion; He was making a divine call for believers to radiate His truth, love, and creativity in a world desperate for light. Yet, for many, this call feels daunting. Fear, often disguised as humility or caution, whispers lies that our talents are too insignificant, too flawed, or too unworthy to make a difference.

This suppression of light creates an environment where the enemy thrives. Spirit spouses and other oppressive forces exploit this fear, isolating individuals and stifling their potential.

This fear is deeply personal and rooted in past experiences that have left us hesitant to step forward. Perhaps as a child, you eagerly shared a dream, only to be met with ridicule or indifference. Maybe you excelled in something, but instead of celebration, it invited envy or scorn from family members. Those wounds linger, shaping the way we see ourselves and the gifts God has entrusted to us. When we dim our light, we miss opportunities to glorify God and bless others. Imagine if Esther, fearing the risks, had chosen silence instead of courage. Her boldness in approaching the king saved an entire nation (Esther 4:14). Or think of David, who, despite being dismissed as just a shepherd boy, stepped forward to face Goliath, bringing victory to Israel (1 Samuel 17).

These stories remind us that our willingness to shine isn't about our own strength or perfection; it's about God's power working through us. The Apostle Paul understood this well, writing, "My grace is sufficient for you, for my power is made perfect in weakness" (2 Corinthians 12:9). Your light isn't meant to be hidden; it's meant to illuminate the darkness. Whether it's a kind word, a creative project, or a bold step of faith, your gifts are uniquely designed to bring hope and healing to others. Isaiah 60:1 declares, "Arise, shine, for your light has come, and the glory of the Lord rises upon you." This isn't a suggestion; it's a commission.

Entertaining Rejection

There was a season in my life where I thought silence was safety. I wouldn't speak my truth, not because the Holy Spirit told me to be quiet, but because fear did. Fear of rejection. Fear of backlash. Fear of being misunderstood. Underneath it all, there was a deep root of unhealed rejection. I began to notice a spiritual pattern. Whenever I chose silence out of fear, I would have dreams where I was eating and every time, those dreams were followed by confusion, exhaustion, or sickness. That wasn't random. It was a spiritual transaction. My obedience to fear opened a door. Revelation 21:8 (ESV) says:

"But as for the cowardly, the faithless, the detestable... their portion will be in the lake that burns with fire..."

That verse used to terrify me until I realized what God was saying. Fear itself isn't the sin, it's what we do with it. We all feel fear; but when we obey fear and choose cowardice instead of courage, silence instead of truth; we step out of agreement with God and into alignment with the enemy. The real turning point in my deliverance was learning to speak up, even with a trembling voice. To say what needed to be said, even when I was afraid. That's when the eating dreams stopped. That's when healing began.

Starving the Spirit: How Neglecting God's Word Feeds Spiritual Battles

Just as the body depends on food for strength and vitality, so does the spirit rely on nourishment from the Word of God to thrive. The Bible isn't just a book; it is divine food, a source of life, wisdom, and power. Yet, when this food is neglected, the spirit becomes weak, vulnerable, and unguarded, opening the door to spiritual battles, including the influence of the spirit spouse, such as eating in dreams.

Spiritual Malnutrition: A Quiet Crisis

Jesus Himself declared in Matthew 4:4, "Man shall not live on bread alone, but on every word that comes from the mouth of God." The Word is described throughout Scripture as essential sustenance: bread, milk, honey, and meat. Yet, in the rush of daily life, it's easy to reduce Scripture to an occasional glance or a hurried devotion. This shallow engagement is like snacking on crumbs when a banquet has been prepared.

When we neglect to "eat" the Word intentionally and regularly, our spirits grow feeble. A weak spirit cannot discern God's voice clearly, resist temptation, or stand firm in spiritual warfare. A hungry spirit is desperate and has space to be fed. It becomes susceptible to the lies of the enemy, who seeks to feed it with doubts, fears, and insecurities. The spirit spouse thrives in these moments, stepping into the void left by spiritual malnutrition to enforce cycles of defeat and despair.

Surface-Level Faith: Nibbling Instead of Feasting

For many, engagement with Scripture is limited to skimming a verse or listening to a sermon. But the Word of God was never meant to be consumed passively. Psalms 1:2-3 paints a picture of the blessed person who "delights in the law of the Lord and meditates on His law day and night." Meditation is like chewing food, breaking it down, digesting it, and allowing it to nourish every body part. Scripture cannot fully take root in our hearts without this deep meditation. A hurried, surface-level approach leaves believers spiritually malnourished, unable to draw on the strength and clarity that God's Word provides.

Nourishing the Spirit

The antidote to spiritual starvation is simple but profound: a return to the Word. Joshua 1:8 reminds us of the transformative power of Scripture: "Keep this Book of the Law always on your lips; meditate on it day and night, so that you may be careful to do everything written in it. Then you will be prosperous and successful." Feeding on the Word isn't just about reading; it's about internalizing. Meditation allows the truths of Scripture to penetrate the heart, empowering believers to walk in freedom and victory. The Word becomes a weapon, sharp and effective, as described in Hebrews 4:12: "For the Word of God is alive and active. Sharper than any double-edged sword, it penetrates even to dividing soul and spirit." When believers prioritize spiritual nourishment, the results are transformative. A well-fed spirit is full of the word and there is no space for it to be fed demonic food like gossip complaining or fear. It is resilient and equipped to stand firm against the enemy's schemes. It is discerning and able to recognize and reject the lies of the spirit spouse. It is also fruitful and flourishing in relationships, purpose, and faith.

Breaking Free from Oppressive Dreams of Eating

1. **a) Confess and Repent:**

    Ask God to reveal any unrepeated sins that may have opened the door to these attacks.

    Break any generational curses through prayer, declaring the victory of Christ over your bloodline.

    b) Identify the lies you have believed and Repent:

    Reflect on the thoughts that hold you back, write them down, and ask God to forgive you for believing them instead of Him. Understand that these thoughts are the voice of an evil spirit that you have chosen to obey and recognize that your decision hurts God's heart. Now, write down their opposites based on God's promises. For example:

The evil spirit says, "You are all alone; you have no help."

You say, "Lord Jesus, forgive me for believing that I am alone. Lord, today I choose to stop believing that I am alone, and I break every covenant that I have made with the spirit of loneliness and the cycle of having no helpers by believing the devil's lie. I cast out of my life and destiny every spirit that came to help accomplish this lie that I believed, and that keeps me alone and without help in Jesus' name. I choose to believe You, Lord, when you say in Isaiah 41:10, "I am with you; I will strengthen you and help you." I look to You, Yahweh, as my first helper and trust that you will send me the help that represents you here on earth."

2. **Step out in faith:**

Take small steps to shine your light, use your gifts, and speak up when you should, trusting God with the consequences of your obedience.

3. **Take Communion & Pray Specifically**

As you take communion, declare:

"As I take this cup of the new covenant in Christ, I superimpose the stipulations of this covenant upon my life. I declare that it nullifies and eradicates every satanic covenant formed through eating in my dreams. I command all circumstances and situations in my life to align with my new covenant with Christ in Jesus' name. Amen."

4. **Guard Your Spiritual Gates**

   Feed your spirit with the Word of God daily. Meditate on His promises and chew on the truth of Scripture. Watch your words, avoiding gossip, complaints, and fear-driven silence.

Tattoos and Incisions: Inviting Spirit Spouses through Body Marks

In contemporary society, tattoos have become a common form of self-expression, often viewed as artistic representations of personal beliefs, memories, or affiliations. However, in many cultures, tattoos and incisions carry deeper spiritual significance, sometimes acting as invitations for spirit spouses to enter a person's life. This phenomenon is rooted in the understanding that our bodies can serve as physical conduits for spiritual entities, making the act of marking the skin a potentially dangerous choice.

Historically, tattoos and incisions have been used in various rituals to signify covenants or alliances with deities, ancestors, or spirits. Where I come from, some children who are plagued by constant infirmity are taken to traditional healers, and cuts are made in their skin for healing. These marks are often believed to carry spiritual weight, acting as symbols of loyalty or servitude to a particular entity, which then specifies which herbs will be placed within the cuts to bring healing to the child. In essence, when an individual receives a tattoo or incision that is rooted in spiritual symbolism or ritualistic practice, they may unknowingly open themselves up to negative spiritual influences like spirit spouses.

The Bible warns against such practices in Leviticus 19:28, which states, "Do not cut your bodies for the dead or put tattoo marks on yourselves. I am the LORD." This directive reflects God's desire for His people to remain separate from practices that could compromise their spiritual integrity. Engaging in tattooing or cutting without a clear understanding of its spiritual implications can lead to unintended consequences, like the summoning of malevolent spirits, including spirit spouses.

Breaking the Bond of Tattoos and Incisions

For those who may feel burdened by the spiritual implications of tattoos or incisions, there are steps to reclaim their spiritual health:

1. **Recognizing the Marks:** The first step is to acknowledge the potential spiritual significance of the tattoos or incisions. This may involve prayerful reflection and seeking God's guidance to understand any links to ancestral practices or spiritual covenants.

2. **Repentance and Renunciation:** Individuals should seek forgiveness for any involvement in practices that may have invited spirit spouses. This may include renouncing any covenants made through the markings and asking God to cleanse them from these spiritual ties.

3. **Prayer for Deliverance:** Engaging in fervent prayer is essential. Ephesians 6:12 reminds us that our struggle is not against flesh and blood, but against spiritual forces. Asking God for deliverance from any negative influences associated with the markings can pave the way for freedom.

4. **Removing or Covering Marks:** In some cases, individuals may choose to remove or cover tattoos that carry negative spiritual significance. This act can serve as a physical manifestation of their desire to break free from past spiritual ties and will be honored by God.

5. **Filling the Void with God's Presence:** It is crucial to fill the space left by the removal of any negative influence with the presence of the Holy Spirit. I suggest anointing the scars from the marks with anointed oil and severing any covenant they represent with demons in the name of Jesus.

Some Additional Open Doors to Repent for to Overcome the Spirit Spouse

To overcome the influence of a spirit spouse, it is crucial to identify and close the spiritual doors that have allowed this entity access to your life. The following are some of the key areas to search your life and repent of:

Unforgiveness: Unforgiveness creates a stronghold that allows the enemy to take residence in our hearts. Ephesians 4:26-27 warns, "In your anger do not sin: Do not let the sun go down while you are still angry, and do not give the devil a foothold." Holding onto grudges not only poisons our souls but also invites spiritual darkness. Forgiveness is a divine act of love and release; when we forgive, we break the enemy's hold and release ourselves into God's freedom.

People-pleasing: Galatians 1:10 declares, "Am I now trying to win the approval of human beings, or of God? Or am I trying to please people? If I were still trying to please people, I would not be a servant of Christ." When we live to please others, we compromise our own identity in Christ. The need for external validation becomes an open door for the enemy, who offers counterfeit approval. Repenting from people-pleasing restores our focus on seeking God's affirmation.

Dressing Immodestly: 1 Timothy 2:9 encourages women to "dress modestly, with decency and propriety." Immodest attire can invite unwanted spiritual attention. Spirit spouses often feed on lust, using this as a foothold to establish unholy bonds. Modesty is not about shame but about respecting the temple of God, which our bodies represent. Dressing modestly shuts the door to the spirit spouse and honors God.

Dressing from a Religious Spirit: Avoiding attractive attire can be rooted in a religious spirit, which is just as harmful as immodesty. Colossians 2:23 warns against false humility and harsh treatment of the body, stating that such practices are of no value in combating sensual indulgence. God desires that we walk in freedom, not in religious bondage. When we dress in a way that honors God and reflects our dignity, we close the door to both extremes' immodesty and legalism.

Staying in Toxic Relationships: Toxic relationships can be a breeding ground for emotional and spiritual manipulation. 1 Corinthians 15:33 says, "Do not be misled: 'Bad company corrupts good character.'" Staying in relationships where we are emotionally, spiritually, or physically harmed opens the door for spirit spouses, as they thrive in environments of dysfunction and pain. Repenting from these relationships allows God to heal us and restore healthy boundaries.

Sexual Sins: Sexual immorality is an open door to spirit spouses. 1 Corinthians 6:18-20 commands us to "Flee from sexual immorality. All other sins a person commits are outside the body, but whoever sins sexually, sins against their own body. Do you not know that your bodies are temples of the Holy Spirit?" Sexual sins, whether they involve kissing, petting, masturbation, or homosexuality, defile the body and create spiritual bonds that can entrap us. Repenting from these sins and seeking deliverance allows us to reclaim the purity that God intended for us.

CHAPTER 3

A Path to Sexual Healing and Wholeness

One of the key signs of a spirit spouse is recurring sexual dreams. Though they may seem pleasurable at first, these dreams often leave the person feeling drained, violated, and spiritually robbed. These encounters are not random; they're often tied to ancestral covenants, aiming to reinforce generational strongholds.

Left unchallenged, the effects can show up in real life as financial struggles, broken relationships, emotional instability, or sexual confusion. The spirit spouse can appear as anyone, even a spouse, child, or animal, often involving acts the victim would never consider in real life. It may even begin tormenting people from childhood, especially through dreams involving homosexuality, incest, or perversion, leading to issues like promiscuity, masturbation, same-sex attraction, or frigidity.

Many suffer silently, bound by shame. God revealed to me that these dreams often point to what I call "**infirmed sexuality**," spiritual wounds rooted in some form of generational sexual sin and unbroken covenants. To break free, we must repent, renounce the sin patterns of our ancestors, and cast out any spirits tied to those covenants. For example:

- If you dream of sex with your child, sibling or parent, repent for ancestral incest.
- If you dream of homosexual acts, confess and renounce generational homosexuality.
- If you're married but dream of having sex with others, break covenants tied to adultery.
- If sex dreams with your spouse feel oppressive, pray for your spouse and break inherited covenants from their bloodline.
- If you dream of exes, sever soul ties and command any attached spirits to leave in Jesus' name.

Sample Prayer

Heavenly Father, I've been tormented by recurring dreams of sexual encounters with my pastor, though I feel no attraction in real life. I lay these dreams at your feet and ask you to shine your light into my soul. Show me any open doors allowing this spirit spouse to operate and give me the strength to close them.

I repent on behalf of myself and my bloodline for any ancestral adultery. I renounce every covenant with the spirit of adultery and break all agreement with it in Jesus' name. I command every demon connected to this sin to leave me and my future generations now.

I seal every portal to my soul with the blood of Jesus. I declare freedom from all spirit spouses rooted in generational sin. In Jesus' mighty name, amen.

My Story

I've personally experienced the torment of a spirit spouse's adulterous dreams. As I cried out to God, He led me to confess and renounce the ancestral sin of adultery, but it didn't stop there. God showed me how I was unknowingly cooperating with this spirit in my present life. At the time, my marriage was strained. My husband wasn't open to spiritual matters, and I was afraid to tell him about my struggles. Instead of taking things to God, I'd run to pastors for deliverance prayers without my husband even knowing. I also made a habit of calling pastors whenever we had problems, rather than seeking God's guidance first. God revealed that these actions were open doors to the enemy. He challenged me with two key steps:

1. Fast from spiritual codependency

The next time I had a disagreement with my husband; I was not to call any pastor. Instead, I was to fast not from food but from that urge to seek people before seeking God (1 Corinthians 7:5). I was to pray, wait for His direction, and only approach a pastor if He clearly led me to.

To my surprise, when I obeyed, God began convicting my husband directly. He would apologize and even grow stronger in the very areas where he'd previously failed me. It was clear God was moving.

2. Bring my husband into the battle

The next instruction was even harder: I had to open up to my husband about my dreams and ask him to pray for me. It started small:

"Honey, I had a bad dream last night. Can you pray for me?"

But over time, as God healed our marriage and my sexuality, I was able to share more, and my husband began to pray with real authority. And it worked. What God was really doing was restoring divine order. God became my first **Shepherd**, Jehovah Rohi (Psalms 23:2). My husband took his rightful place as my **covering and priest**. Pastors became supplemental, not primary spiritual support. This alignment brought a tremendous breakthrough in my deliverance journey. I couldn't have done it without first allowing God to heal my wounded sexuality. That healing gave me the courage to bring my husband into the fight, and that's where real victory began.

Sexual Healing

Healing your sexuality is a journey into God's original design. In a world filled with distorted messages about sexuality, it's easy to lose sight of the truth that God created our sexuality as a beautiful part of our humanity. This chapter is about rediscovering that truth and embracing the healing God desires for each of us.

The Bible tells us that our bodies are sacred: "Do you not know that your bodies are temples of the Holy Spirit, who is in you, whom you have received from God? You are not your own; you were bought at a price. Therefore, honor God with your bodies" (1 Corinthians 6:19-20). God designed sexuality as a gift to be experienced in ways that align with His divine purposes. Yet, many of us have encountered pain, shame, or confusion in this area, whether due to past experiences, personal struggles, or spiritual influences like spirit spouses that seek to disrupt and distort.

To heal our sexuality, we must go to the root wounds that bring about these personal struggles. As you walk through this chapter, know that this journey is both sacred and deeply personal. True healing requires courage, honesty, and the willingness to let God work in areas we may have kept hidden. Embracing this process means choosing to see yourself as God sees you, to let go of guilt, and to walk confidently in His love.

Together, let's take this journey. Allow yourself to receive God's love and restoration, to experience a freedom that lifts shame and breathes new life into your heart. Remember, you're not alone. As you heal, you're aligning with God's blueprint and opening yourself to the fullness of life He designed for you.

Understanding God's Design for Sexuality

God's design for sexuality is beautifully intricate and deeply rooted in His purpose for humanity. At its core, sexuality is a gift meant to be experienced within the sacred covenant of marriage, where intimacy serves as a profound expression of love, connection, and unity. When we look at Scripture, we find that God established this design not only for procreation but also for the deepening of the marital bond, a bond that reflects His relationship with His people. In Genesis 2:24 (NIV), we see the foundation of this divine design: "That is why a man leaves his father and mother and is united to his wife, and they become one flesh." This verse proves that the essence of marital sexual intimacy is a coming together that transcends the physical to create a spiritual bond of unity.

Healthy sexual intimacy serves several purposes in marriage:

1. **Connection:** Sexual intimacy cultivates a deep emotional connection, allowing partners to share their innermost thoughts and feelings. This bond creates an atmosphere of trust and safety, which is essential for a flourishing relationship.

2. **Joy:** Sexual intimacy is meant to be an expression of joy and delight. The Song of Solomon beautifully illustrates this: "Let my beloved come into his garden and taste its choice fruits" (Songs of Solomon 4:16). Such expressions celebrate the joy found in mutual pleasure and love.

3. **Defense Against Spiritual Intrusions:** Sexual intimacy within a godly marriage acts as a barrier against spiritual attacks, particularly from spirit spouses that seek to disrupt and distort the marital bond.

The Spiritual Significance of Sex

The significance of sex embodies a spiritual principle wherein two souls become one in Christ. Ephesians 5:31-32 beautifully captures this truth: "For this reason, a man will leave his father and mother and be united to his wife, and the two will become one flesh. This is a profound mystery but I am talking about Christ and the church." In this passage, the Apostle Paul unveils the divine mystery of marriage as a sacred reflection of Christ's unwavering love for the church, illuminating the reality that marital intimacy is not just a physical act but also a deeply spiritual union that encapsulates God's covenantal love.

So, we see that in the spirit realm, **sex is never only between two people; it is between two people and a spirit. When the sexual act is performed under the confines of marriage, the spirit that accompanies it is the spirit of Yahweh, but when it is not done within the confines of marriage, the spirit that accompanies it is a demonic spirit. This is because God will never endorse what He does not permit.** In a world that often trivializes physical relationships, this biblical perspective invites us to reclaim the beauty and sanctity of intimacy. It challenges us to view our bodies as temples of the Holy Spirit, reminding us that every intimate encounter is an opportunity to honor God and reflect His glory, and also reminding us to be careful. Whenever you choose to have sex, you are enforcing a marriage-like covenant with a spirit. It can either be with the spirit of God or with a demonic spirit, based on who you choose to have sex with. The choice is yours; choose wisely! (Deuteronomy 30:19).

Understanding the Root Causes of Sexual Infirmity

Many of the things we label as sexual sin like homosexuality, lesbianism, or pornography are often rooted in sexual infirmity, not just rebellion. These are wounds, not just choices. And when those wounds go unhealed, they can solidify into strongholds of sin. At the core is often a shame-based sexuality, a distorted identity formed through trauma, rejection, or early exposure to perversion. Similarly, societal pressures and unrealistic portrayals of sexuality in the media can contribute to the development of these issues without healing, shame becomes the lens through which people see themselves, and sin becomes the cycle they can't escape.

In confronting these issues, self-reflection becomes paramount. Individuals should take time to identify their trigger situations, emotions, or environments that led them to seek out unhealthy sexual outlets. Taking a trip down memory lane into the relationships modeled around us as children, while keeping a journal, can be a powerful tool in this process, allowing individuals to track their thoughts, feelings, and behaviors. Over time, this can reveal patterns that need to be addressed and provide insight into the emotional pain that often fuels sexual infirmity.

Where Identity and Sexuality Take Root

Whether we realize it or not, the environment we create in our marriages directly influences the next generation's sexual health. When children witness their parents living in unity, offering love, and practicing healthy conflict resolution, they are learning not just about romance but about sacrifice, compromise, and the deep care that God intended for marriage. This is how godly offspring are raised, as Malachi 2:15 reminds us: "Has not the one God made you? You belong to him in body and spirit. And what does the one God seek? Godly offspring." The purpose of marriage goes beyond the couples. It is about raising a generation that will carry on the principles of the Kingdom.

If a child grows up seeing their parents' commitment to one another, they'll learn what it means to be in a committed relationship, reflecting God's love and covenant with His people. But when that environment is absent, or if marriage is marked by discord, anger, or neglect, children are left to wrestle with confusion about what love and sexual identity really mean.

Dysfunctional marriages lead to dysfunctional family systems which are open doors to spirit spouses and their child, called Sexual Infirmity. You see, they thrive in homes where there is no male figure who stands as a spiritual leader and spiritual covering submitted to Jesus Christ. A father's absence, whether emotional or physical, leaves a void. For example, a boy child may grow up without a clear understanding of what it means to be a man or how a man should treat women and thus turn to homosexuality in an attempt to feel the intimacy he missed from his father and cope with not knowing how to treat a woman. A mother's harsh words or withdrawal of affection can also create lasting emotional scars, leading her daughter into lesbianism because she finds herself yearning for female love and intimacy. These experiences shape the way children view themselves and what kind of sexual partners they will be attracted to. A daughter may struggle with self-worth if she observes her mother being disrespected or ignored. A son may grapple with what it means to be a husband who is emotionally available for his wife if he never witnesses it firsthand. Every choice parents make, every moment of care or neglect, plants seeds that will later bear fruit in the child's sexuality.

When Talking About Sex Was Forbidden

For some individuals, sexual issues stem from a much larger cultural or familial silence around sex. Imagine a young girl, curious and innocent, asking her parents a question about love, marriage, or her changing body. Instead of receiving an honest and thoughtful answer, she's met with anger, scorn, or even punishment.

"Don't ask such things again!"

"Good girls don't talk about that!"

These moments leave a mark. To a child, such reactions send a clear message: sex is **wrong, dirty, or dangerous**. This shame doesn't vanish with time; it follows her into adulthood, becoming her identity, and this can transform into a silent barrier in her marriage. Some parents, uncomfortable with the topic, might not resort to punishment but instead give vague or misleading answers. For example, a child might ask, "Where do babies come from?" only to be told, "You'll understand when you're older," or "Don't think about that." While these answers might seem harmless, they teach the child that curiosity about sex is something to suppress.

In more extreme cases, like in my country of origin, Cameroon, practices such as **breast ironing** are implemented. This is the pounding and massaging of a pubescent girl's breasts, using hard or heated objects to try to make them stop developing or disappear. Also, in some parts of Africa, including my country, Cameroon, and Kenya, many girls between the ages of 9 and 15 undergo **female genital mutilation (FGM)**, the cutting of the clitoris and labia in the name of purity or tradition.

These practices are typically performed by a close female figure to the victim, traditionally fulfilled by a mother, grandmother, aunt, or female guardian who will say she is trying to protect the girl from early sexual practices or sexual harassment to prevent early pregnancy that would tarnish the family name. The girls are told it will make them clean or worthy of marriage, but it often leads to deep pain, shame, and trauma.

These harsh responses instill a fear of discussing sex openly, one that lingers well into marriage. Individuals with this kind of background often find it hard to communicate their sexual desires or needs to their spouses. They might feel embarrassed or ashamed, even when they deeply want to connect, and this can open the door to a spirit spouse offering them sexual satisfaction in their dreams in exchange for frigidity in their marriage.

In many Christian homes, the silence around sex can inadvertently teach children that it's a subject that God is not pleased with and to be ashamed of. Instead, we need to create an environment where open, honest conversations can take place where sex is acknowledged as a beautiful, God-given gift that deserves respect, honor, and understanding. These conversations don't have to be uncomfortable or awkward; they should be filled with truth and grace, helping the next generation understand the importance of sexuality in light of God's love and design. When we do this, we break the chains of shame and build a foundation of truth that will empower our children to approach their sexuality with maturity and respect.

Sex is not the enemy. The enemy is shame, the silence, and the lies that have surrounded it and that open the doors to spirit spouses tormenting our generations long after we are gone. Let's communicate to our children that sex is a gift from God and celebrate it as God intended, so we do not leave our children open to sexual sin.

Shame Based Sexuality

I have concluded in my deliverance journey and through counseling many individuals that most sexual sin is rooted in the sin of **a shame-based sexuality**, as discussed above. You see, when we label what God has created as "shameful" or "bad," we are attaching negativity to our creator and inviting perverting demons to bring to pass the very thing we are trying to avoid. Most sexual sin usually starts as sexual curiosity. When the outlet for sexual curiosity has gotten apart from the way God created it to be (which is progressive, parental, age-appropriate discussions), it can open the door for sexual sin. That said, this is not an excuse to stay in patterns of sexual sin. It is important to remember that engaging in sexual acts outside the divine context of marriage can create spiritual vulnerabilities that allow demonic spirits like spirit spouses to take root and exert their influence.

The Bible is clear about the consequences of immorality and the importance of maintaining purity. 1 Corinthians 6:18-20 admonishes us, stating, "Flee from sexual immorality. All other sins a person commits are outside the body, but whoever sins sexually, sins against their own body. Do you not know that your bodies are temples of the Holy Spirit, who is in you, whom you have received from God? You are not your own; you were bought at a price. Therefore, honor God with your bodies." This passage highlights not only the severity of sexual sin but also its unique nature in that it directly affects our bodies, which are meant to be sanctuaries for the Holy Spirit. When we engage in sexual immorality, we not only violate God's design for human sexuality but also expose ourselves to **sexual infirmity.** We see how this can create a never-ending cycle which evil spirits can exploit. Proverbs 6:32 warns, "But a man who commits adultery has no sense; whoever does so destroys himself." The Scripture reflects the self-destructive nature of sexual immorality. Engaging in such behavior opens doors not only to personal pain but also to generational curses that can affect family lines. This is often seen in families where cycles of immorality are repeated, perpetuating the influence of spirit spouses through ancestral ties.

Masturbation: The Bait of the Spirit Spouse

It often starts with curiosity, a moment of discovery in the silence of youth. No one talks to you about your body or God's purpose for it. So when pleasure stirs unexpectedly, in a bath, a bedroom, or a moment alone, it feels like a secret gift, innocent and exciting. A whisper says, "It's your body, your choice." But what seems harmless can become a doorway. Behind pleasure is a spiritual law: it was created to bond two souls under God's covenant. Outside of that, it invites something else, a spirit with legal grounds to enter.

Lila was 19, committed to purity, yet stumbled upon self-pleasure by accident. It became a secret escape, then a silent addiction. At first, it felt like safety from a chaotic home and unmet emotional needs. But the pleasure gave way to guilt.

She noticed a dark presence lingering after each episode, something unseen, heavy, and cold. Friends dismissed her guilt: "You're still a virgin. There's no harm." Even her mother wouldn't talk about it. And so, Lila continued, unaware that her soul had made room for a generational spirit spouse.

By her mid-twenties, Lila was married but couldn't enjoy intimacy. The pleasure she once controlled now controlled her. She cried out to God one cold night, desperate and broken, "If you see me, set me free." It wasn't polished, but it was real. Something shifted. Her healing didn't come overnight. God began to reveal that sexual pleasure outside of marriage isn't just a physical act; it's a spiritual invitation. She learned that masturbation opens doors for unclean spirits. As she repented, studied the Word, and sought God as her healer, she began to break free.

God showed her that pleasure isn't bad; it's sacred. But when misused, it attracts bondage. Lila's chain broke when truth replaced the lie: she wasn't dirty or broken, just misled. God's love cut through her shame. The presence that tormented her left, and peace took its place.

Lila's story isn't rare. For many, masturbation begins as an innocent act but becomes a gateway to pornography and deeper bondage. Though the Bible doesn't mention the word "masturbation," it warns against impurity and sensuality (Galatians 5:19). These behaviors distort God's design for sex and intimacy. But there's hope. God's design is not restrictive; it's redemptive. Pleasure is His gift, meant to be shared in covenant love, guarded by His Spirit. When we cry out, He hears. Freedom is possible, not because we are strong, but because He is.

Pornography: A Symptom and a Doorway to Spirit Spouses.

For many people trapped in the cycle of pornography, the entry point wasn't a conscious decision. Lucas's story is a tender example of this. Lucas was a 14-year-old boy growing up in a quiet village in Africa. He had a good heart, a playful spirit, and a deep desire to understand the world around him. However, like many children, he had no one to walk him through the beauty and boundaries of God's design for sexuality. In his home, the subject was never brought up; not out of neglect, but because it was considered inappropriate or taboo to talk about such things with children.

One day, while playing near a row of homes made of thin wooden planks, known locally as carabot houses, Lucas overheard unfamiliar sounds. Thinking someone might be in pain, he looked through a gap in the boards. What he witnessed was his first exposure to adult intimacy. In that moment, three things settled in his soul: confusion, shame and pleasure. Though he didn't understand what he saw, and it deeply unsettled him, his body reacted. Without consent or comprehension, his body awakened to something his mind and heart were not prepared for. He felt the physical sensation of pleasure mixed with the emotional discomfort of secrecy, fear, and shame and because no one had ever talked to him about these things, he didn't know what to do with any of it. Unable to process what had happened, Lucas turned to an older friend, hoping to make sense of it. That friend, also too young to carry such weight, introduced Lucas to magazines and tapes. And so began a quiet spiral. What started as a moment of curiosity became a habit of secrecy, and eventually a stronghold.

By the time Lucas was an adult, pornography was a part of his life he couldn't seem to escape. It brought fleeting relief from stress but left him with lasting guilt and heaviness he could not shake. Soon he was having repeated sexual dreams which left him drained and operating with recurring fits of rage.

Overcoming Patterns of Sexual Infirmity

Many people who struggle with adultery or fornication or engage in pornography, masturbation, or any other sexual sin may feel trapped in a cycle of shame and guilt. The spirit spouse can exacerbate these feelings, whispering lies that reinforce a sense of unworthiness, hopelessness, and separation from God's love. It may whisper lies like, "This is how you are; you can never change; you are a malfunction." Understanding that these feelings are often rooted in spiritual warfare can empower individuals to take action against them.

Overcoming any form of sexual brokenness requires a deep exploration of one's identity, values, and the underlying wounds that may have contributed to these feelings. It is essential to seek healing from past traumas, rejection, or negative experiences that have shaped one's perception of love and acceptance. This journey often involves seeking counsel from trusted mentors, engaging in supportive communities, and, most importantly, immersing oneself in the truth of Scripture.

Romans 12:2 urges us not to conform to the patterns of this world but to be transformed by the renewing of our minds. This transformation is crucial for anyone seeking freedom from unwanted sexual desires or habits. By intentionally engaging with God's Word, individuals can begin to rewrite their narratives, replacing lies with truths about their identity as beloved children of God.

1. Acknowledging the Impact of the Past

The first step toward healing is acknowledging how past experiences impact your current life. Sexual sin influenced by spirit spouses can often be traced back to unresolved traumas and distorted views of oneself. Recognizing that these experiences do not define you is crucial; they may have shaped your journey, but they do not dictate your worth or your future. By acknowledging the pain and its role in your life, you can begin taking the necessary steps toward healing. Don't be afraid to let yourself sit with the pain and cry as you pour your heart out to God or a trusted individual. This recognition and purging of trapped negative emotions can be a catalyst for breaking the strongholds of spirit spouses, allowing you to reclaim your identity and your sexual health.

2. Repentance: Freedom through God's Grace

The prayer of repentance is a powerful tool in this journey. Perhaps as you read this chapter, you have discovered that, indeed, your sexual issues stem from a generational shame-based view of sexuality. Start with deep repentance on behalf of yourself and your generational line for adopting **"a shame-based sexuality."**

Next, repent for any sexual sin you may have engaged in. For example, if frigidity has made you deny sexual intimacy to your spouse, ask God to forgive you for disobeying His command in 1 Corinthians 7:5, which states, "Do not deprive each other except perhaps by mutual consent and for a time, so that you may devote yourselves to prayer. Then come together again so that Satan will not tempt you because of your lack of self-control."

Healing involves understanding the depth of God's grace. Embracing the concept that God sees you not through the lens of your mistakes but through His love can be transformative. This perspective shift enables you to reclaim your identity and move toward healing, effectively closing the door on the spirit spouse that seeks to dominate your life.

3. The Role of Self-Forgiveness

Self-forgiveness is a vital element in the healing process. Many who struggle with sexual addiction often grapple with guilt and shame, especially when confronting influences from spirit spouses that may distort their sexual identity. Understand that while acknowledging past mistakes is important, clinging to guilt can keep you trapped in cycles of unhealthy behavior.

God's grace offers a path to freedom. Reflecting on Scriptures like 1 John 1:9 reminds us that if we confess our sins, He is faithful and just and will forgive us. Embracing this truth can help dismantle the walls of shame and guilt that spirit spouses thrive upon, allowing for healing and restoration. Consider articulating your feelings about past choices and how they have affected your life. Write a letter to yourself, acknowledging your pain and mistakes but also affirming your worth in God's eyes. This exercise can be a profound step toward embracing self-forgiveness and releasing the burden of shame, which is often a gateway for spirit spouses to continue to exert influence.

4. Establishing Healthy Boundaries

Once individuals gain insight into their triggers, establishing healthy boundaries is crucial in overcoming sexual issues. This may involve limiting exposure to certain environments, media, or even relationships that encourage unhealthy behaviors. For example, filtering internet content can help remove temptations associated with pornography. Individuals might also consider taking breaks from social media platforms where unrealistic portrayals of relationships and bodies can trigger feelings of inadequacy or desire. Sometimes, spirit spouses can be reinforced by unhealthy relationships or toxic environments that lead you back into patterns of addiction. It's essential to identify these triggers and make the necessary changes.

5. Engaging in Support Networks

Support networks are vital in the journey toward healing. Whether through church groups, therapy, or support groups. Connecting with others who understand the struggle can provide immense comfort and encouragement. Women struggling with a lack of sexual desire for their husbands can join a women's ministry and confide in other older and more experienced ladies who might be able to offer godly advice and pray for their desire toward their husbands to be restored. These groups often offer a safe space to share experiences and struggles, fostering a sense of community and belonging, and can help relieve anxiety and depression, which are often associated with sexual issues.

6. Engaging in Therapy or Counseling

Through therapy, you can unpack the complex emotions and past traumas that have shaped your view of self and sexuality. This process of exploration can be liberating, allowing you to confront painful memories and begin to rewrite your narrative. You'll gain valuable coping strategies and skills to manage your emotions, helping you navigate the tumultuous waters of recovery.

7. Establishing New Habits

Replacing negative behaviors with positive ones is crucial in the journey toward healing. Individuals should actively seek out activities that promote personal growth, fulfillment, and healthy relationships. This could involve pursuing hobbies, volunteering, or investing time in meaningful friendships that uplift and encourage.

Physical exercise can also be an effective way to cope with the urges associated with sexual addiction. Engaging in regular physical activity not only releases endorphins, natural mood lifters, but also helps individuals channel their energy into constructive outlets. Furthermore, exercise can be a powerful way to rebuild body image and self-esteem, countering the negative self-perceptions often exacerbated by sexual addiction.

For those who struggle with sexual frigidity within marriage, it is important to look into underlying traumatic associations one has had with the concept of sex and develop the habit to talk openly to your partner about this. Engage in a deliberate time of prayer and ask God for wisdom on how to make sex fun and satisfying in your marriage. Establishing new habits like taking a nice bubble bath and lighting some scented candles before the actual sexual act might help. Find creative ways with your partner to start associating sex with what you consider positive aspects of life. The goal here is not to fall into the temptation of accepting frigidity as part of your married life. You need as much healing, deliverance, and accountability as the individual struggling with pornography within the marriage, and this is especially true if you are getting sexually satisfying dreams with a spirit spouse. As you begin to be deliberate in doing the work it takes to associate sex within your marriage with a positive atmosphere, you will find that the spirit spouse dreams within which you are getting sexual satisfaction will come to an end, and you will be able to experience real-life pleasure with your spouse.

8. Reclaiming Your God-Given Identity

Reclaiming your identity means embracing the fullness of who God created you to be. This process involves both self-reflection and active engagement in practices that reinforce your identity in Christ:

a. Daily Prayer and Meditation

Every morning, as the sun rises, take a moment to quiet your heart and connect with God. Begin your day in prayer, inviting His presence into your life and acknowledging your need for His guidance. In those quiet moments, lay your struggles before Him, especially the areas where spirit spouses have sought to bind you. Reflect on Scripture that affirms your worth and identity. Verses like 1 John 3:1 remind you of God's love for you when it states, "See what great love the Father has lavished on us, that we should be called children of God!" This truth is your anchor, grounding you as you face the challenges of the day.

b. Identifying Gifts and Passions: Take time to explore your unique gifts and passions. What activities bring you joy? What are your strengths? One of the most effective ways to break free from the grip of sexual sin is to redirect the energy behind it. Sexual desire is powerful but it's not evil. It was created by God and, when surrendered to Him, that same intensity can be channeled into something holy. Many people battling pornography and masturbation feel overwhelmed by urges they can't seem to control, but what if that drive could be poured into your God-given gifts and passions? Whether it's writing, building, creating, serving, or leading. When you begin to pour yourself into your purpose, you'll find that the very energy once used to feed lust can instead ignite destiny.

9. Seeking Accountability

In the journey of healing, accountability is a gift. Seek out a trusted friend, mentor, or support group who understands your struggles. This relationship should be built on trust, love, and a shared commitment to growth. Regular check-ins can provide you with the encouragement you need to stay focused and motivated. Sharing your battles openly can diminish the power of shame that spirit spouses often exploit. These individuals can offer encouragement, prayer, and a safe space to process feelings and experiences without judgment. They can also hold one accountable, helping to navigate temptations and fostering a sense of belonging that is often sought in unhealthy relationships. When you expose darkness to the light, you'll find that you are not alone in your struggles.

That's why I created the virtual **Monday Prayer Room**. This is a safe, judgment-free space for people who are walking through deliverance from spirit spouses. We meet every Monday (except the last Monday of the month) on Google Meet. Those who attend have experienced the pain and spiritual warfare that come with these types of bondages. In this space, we share intimate details, pray deeply, interpret dreams, and encourage one another in the light of God's truth. Some even come with struggles related to homosexuality, and we lovingly stand with them in prayer and healing. Many have found breakthroughs and peace simply by knowing they are not alone.

10. Embracing Turning Points in the Healing Journey

Specific turning points can significantly influence the healing journey. These moments can be small yet powerful, such as insightful conversations, impactful sermons, or profound moments of prayer. Recognizing these turning points provides hope and motivation, encouraging you to continue seeking healing and closing the door to spirit spouses. Set aside time for self-reflection to identify pivotal moments that brought about change. Consider what experiences shifted your perspective and guided you toward healing. Documenting these insights can reinforce your progress and remind you of the steps you've taken toward reclaiming your life from the grasp of spirit spouses.

Stop the Transgenerational Spirit Spouse for Good!

You are defeating the generational spirit spouse. You are healing your sexuality and shattering invisible cages that have trapped you for years. But make no mistake, demons are stubborn. When they lose you, they look for your children. They come for the next generation, the seed of your destiny, and the main doorway they seek is premarital sex. Understand this: whoever controls a child's understanding of sexuality controls their destiny gates; their marriage, ministry, fruitfulness, identity, and even mental health. The enemy knows that if he can corrupt your child's sexual understanding early, he doesn't have to fight their prayers later. They'll sabotage themselves without even knowing it.

Why You Must Be the First Voice About Sex

First Voice = Lasting Authority

The first time a child learns about any sacred subject, it builds a default setting in their mind. Whatever version of truth they receive first becomes the lens through which they filter every other experience. If you are the first to speak about sex, they will always measure the world's lies against the truth you gave.

If a perverted world speaks first, your words will seem like outdated rules, not life-saving truths. In the courts of Heaven, parenting isn't just provision and education; it's stewardship of souls. When you remain silent about sexuality because of awkwardness, shame, or fear, the enemy interprets your silence as consent to indoctrinate them himself. He will send cartoons, predators, feelings, and dreams. Your child, out of natural curiosity, will sit at the enemy's feet to learn because you refused to speak.

How to Introduce Sex to Your Child God's Way

This is not a one-time talk. It's a lifetime conversation built in stages, on truth and love, with warfare wisdom backing every word.

Stage 1: Innocence & Identity (Ages 3–7)

- ❖ Teach them that their bodies are sacred.
- ❖ Use correct names for private parts; don't make it weird or shameful.
- ❖ Begin blessing their bodies in prayer: Tell them, "You are fearfully and wonderfully made. Your body is holy."
- ❖ Anoint them with oil occasionally and decree protection over their body, mind, and dreams.

Stage 2: Curiosity & Boundaries (Ages 8–10)

- ❖ Introduce God's idea of love, marriage, and sexual intimacy.
- ❖ Teach that private parts are for private places and only for their future spouse under God's covenant.

- ❖ Practice "open table" talks; no question is taboo. You must be their safest teacher.
- ❖ Every night, bind spirits of early sexual awakening and dream molestation and cancel any assignments.

The 8th Birthday Box: A Rite of Passage

When my daughters turn eight, I mark the occasion with a special "Growing Up Box." It's a beautiful, symbolic way to begin a more direct conversation about the changes their bodies will experience and to introduce the topic of sex in a clear, sacred, and age-appropriate way.

Here's what I include in the box:

- ❖ A small pack of sanitary pads: A gift to prepare her for her first period, which she keeps in her schoolbag daily. My first period came while I was at school, and I had no idea what was happening to me or what to do. I stayed with soaked underwear until I got home. It ends with me!
- ❖ Lip gloss and body spray (to represent self-love and self-care).
- ❖ Mints (to represent fresh words and kindness).

103

❖ A laminated copy of Isaiah 54:5, "For your Maker is your Husband; the Lord Almighty is his name."

We go out together, just the two of us, for our first trip to the nail salon, and I use this time to make her feel cherished, seen, and celebrated. It's not just about growing up. It's about being covered in truth before the world has a chance to lie.

When we sit down for the talk, I begin by asking,

"What do you already know about where babies come from or what sex is?" This allows me to listen first to find out what information (or misinformation) has already made its way to their ears. I then explain sex honestly but respectfully, in a biologically accurate yet spiritually anchored way. I tell them:

"Sex is when a man's penis goes into a woman's vagina. It feels good because God made it that way for bonding and for creating children. But He also made it to be protected inside marriage so that it's safe, holy, and deeply meaningful."

If your child has already been exposed to things too early, don't panic. Start from where they are, not where you wish they were. They don't need shame; they need clarity, safety, and truth. Next, I share Isaiah 54:5 with my daughters and give them the laminated Scripture. I say to them:

"Before you ever get married to a person, you already belong to someone. God is your first Husband. He is your protector. He watches over your body, your heart, and even your dreams."

Then, I gently open up the conversation about spirit spouses. I tell them, **"Just like God is your Husband and wants to protect you, there's a spirit that tries to pretend to be a husband or a wife, too. But it's not from God. This spirit tries to sneak in through dreams or thoughts to confuse you, touch you, or lie to you. It wants to pervert what God made beautiful. That's not okay, and you don't have to accept it."** I let them know clearly, **"If you ever have a dream where someone is touching your private parts or doing anything sexual, that is not from God. Your body is too holy for that. Come tell me, and we'll pray together. We won't be afraid, and we won't be ashamed. God delivers. He did it for Mommy, and He will do it for you."**

By connecting Isaiah 54:5 to this part of the conversation, I help my children understand that intimacy belongs to God first and that no spirit has the right to take that place. It's not about fear; it's about truth. It's about covering their minds and hearts before the enemy tries to sow lies and confusion.

You don't have to follow this example exactly. What matters is intentionality. Make it special, memorable, and God-centered. And most of all, keep the conversation open and ongoing, and let your own sexual healing show by the fact that you don't look ashamed as you speak. Keep a smile on your face and do your best to talk about all of this just like you were explaining how to use the toilet. It may be difficult for you, just as it was for me, but remember, you are the curse breaker; you have never seen or experienced what God is asking you to do. God is proud of you, and He is with you to help you.

Stage 3: Awareness & War (Ages 12–14)

- ❖ Before puberty hits, explain it clearly: changes in the body, emotions, and urges.
- ❖ Talk about real threats: masturbation, pornography, peer pressure, and molestation.
- ❖ Warn them: let them know that not everything that feels good is good because some things open spiritual cages.
- ❖ Help them build their own private prayer altar. Teach them to cover themselves daily.
- ❖ Start encouraging them to pray for their spouse to be.

Stage 4: Legacy & Destiny (Ages 14–17)

❖ Talk more openly about soul ties, sexual urges, attraction to the opposite sex, and spiritual covenants made through sex.

❖ Share testimonies. It is important that you share your mistakes (with wisdom), share your victories, too. Show them that purity is power, not punishment. Help them redirect their passions toward manifesting their gifts and talents and serving at the local church.

❖ Have them memorize Scriptures that wage war over purity (e.g., 1 Corinthians 6:18–20, 1 Thessalonians 4:3–5).

❖ Do prayer fasts with them once a month for their destiny protection. Continue to encourage them to pray against marriage delays and to pray real prayers for their spouse.

❖ Encourage them to make a small list of what they want in a spouse and to lift that list to God in prayer. Children are naturally imaginative. Why not direct that imagination toward faith instead of lustful fantasy. You can even write out a prayer with your child, put it in a little envelope or journal, and revisit it together every year. Let them see their faith grow as they grow. Let them hope, not just abstain. Here is a sample prayer:

"Heavenly Father, please protect my future husband/wife today. Help him love you with all his heart. Keep his eyes and body pure. Surround him with wise friends and help him grow strong in his faith. Thank You that You are preparing me and preparing him, and thank You that you will help us to meet each other at the right time and have a beautiful wedding."

When your child knows that there's a real spouse being prepared for them and that they are being prepared in return, they won't see themselves as alone in the fight. They will see themselves as connected, chosen, and worth waiting for. You're not just helping them say "no" to temptation; you're helping them say "yes" to the future God is writing.

CHAPTER 4

Marriage: The primary target of the spirit spouse

Most people who are in a battle with the spirit spouse can attest to the fact that its primary method of operating against them has been surrounding the issue of relationships. This is especially true when it comes to marriage. There's a reason why the devil hates marriage. It is the foundation of godly generations. A strong, Christ-centered marriage is a threat to the kingdom of darkness because it produces children who know who they are in Christ and are equipped to fulfill their purpose.

Satan understands that if he can destroy the family, he can destroy the foundation of society. He uses every tool at his disposal—divorce, infidelity, selfishness, and societal redefinitions of marriage—to undermine God's design.

My Story

The spirit spouse was determined to keep me from getting married. By the special grace of God, in spite of the regular spirit spouse sexual encounters in my dream, I was able to overcome through intense prayer and fasting. However, two years into my marriage, I began to feel a shift in my relationship that I couldn't ignore. It was as though my husband and I had become strangers, living in the same space but emotionally distant, like roommates rather than a married couple.

During this time, I started experiencing even more disturbing sexual encounters with this spirit spouse. These encounters were not physical, yet they left me feeling drained, bound to my bedroom, and frigid toward my husband. I would wake up in the morning, feeling weighed down by an overwhelming sense of doom and despair. At some point, I even felt suicidal. The thought of taking a shower, of cleansing myself, became unbearable. It was as if this spirit spouse had marked me and made me feel unworthy of love or care. Every time I tried to care for myself, whether it was grooming, dressing up, or even trying to feel beautiful, it felt like the weight of something unseen was holding me back.

I prayed and sought God, desperate for His guidance. Then, I heard His still, quiet voice instructing me: "Buy a particular perfume, fast, pray, and anoint your home, including your shower, with oil." As strange as it seemed, I obeyed. I went out and bought the specific perfume God had told me to get. I later realized that God was calling me through the buying of the perfume to reclaim my self-care, which I had abandoned due to depression. I followed His instructions to the letter. I anointed the entire house, including the bathroom, where I had begun to feel the evil spirit's presence most acutely. I used the oil, not just as a physical act, but as a spiritual act of warfare, asking God to cleanse me and my home (Isaiah 10:27). Then, God's answer came some days later during my time of prayer. God opened my eyes to the revelation of how the strongman spirit spouse had been manipulating my family line through the years in the area of marriage. When I understood this, I began to fight for change, not from the desire to keep my current marriage but from the desire to have a godly marriage.

But let me be clear: **a restored marriage isn't the only measure of true deliverance**. Deliverance is about transformation. And sometimes, your marriage won't survive that transformation, especially if your spouse chooses not to grow with you. They may have been drawn to who you used to be. Loving the healed, redeemed version of you will require their own surrender, growth, and spiritual maturity. God will not override their free will. Consider Shanna's story:

Shanna was deeply committed to her marriage but always sensed something was off. Her husband, Michael, was emotionally distant and spiritually absent. She tried everything to keep the relationship alive, but it was one-sided. She constantly walked on eggshells, craving connection, while he remained passive. It wasn't until Shanna began her deliverance journey that she uncovered a deeper truth. Her intense need to fix, please, and rescue wasn't just emotional; it was spiritual. A spirit spouse had forged a soul tie with her identity, making her equate love with performance and rejection with failure. She was bound to broken patterns that had been modeled for her.

Her mother had been married to a man just like Michael: detached, unavailable, and uninterested in spiritual leadership. Over time, her mother hardened. She built walls to protect herself, becoming emotionally distant, manipulative, and bitter. What began as survival eventually turned into subtle narcissism. The spirit spouse used her pain to create a counterfeit strength rooted in self-preservation. Her auntie, on the other hand, went the opposite direction. Faced with the same neglect, she tried even harder to be accepted. She overserved, avoided conflict, and became addicted to approval. Her emotional exhaustion led to physical fainting spells, anxiety, and mental breakdowns. She never felt good enough and constantly tried to earn love. The spirit spouse exploited her people-pleasing to keep her enslaved. Shanna was standing at the same fork in the road. Would she become bitter and controlling like her mother? Would she collapse into self-abandonment like her auntie? Or would she rise as the curse breaker? God showed her that the real battle wasn't just for her marriage; it was for her identity. God called her to wholeness, not performance. She chose to stop chasing her husband's validation and became the spiritual leader of her own atmosphere. She built boundaries, invested in her healing, and stopped apologizing for her growth. Michael never changed; he became abusive, and Shanna had to get a divorce. Shanna stopped begging to be loved and started living loved. That was the breakthrough.

Unlike Shanna, I was blessed that my marriage was restored. Not because I fought harder but because by God's grace my husband was willing to grow, too. God honored my obedience and our mutual willingness to align with His design for marriage. If you're the one God wakes up first, don't be discouraged. He often calls the more spiritually awake spouse to stand in the gap. "For the unbelieving husband has been sanctified through his wife" (1 Corinthians 7:14). God desires restoration not just for comfort, but for legacy.

How the Spirit Spouse Destroys Marriages

In order to understand why marriages crumble, it is crucial to look at both the tangible and spiritual factors at play. Spirit spouses are often a hidden factor in this breakdown. Recognizing the existence of these spiritual forces and how their operations manifest physically when it comes to marriage relationships is the first step in combating their influence and restoring the sanctity and unity of marriage.

1. Unequally Yoked

One of the subtle yet destructive ways the spirit spouse gains access is through the desperation for marriage, especially when that desperation leads to disobedience. Many believers, weary from waiting, let their guard down and marry someone who has not surrendered their life to Christ. At first, it may seem manageable, but over time, the cracks show. You realize you're not on the same page spiritually. Your value systems clash. Things like prayer, church, purity and forgiveness which you consider sacred become optional or offensive to them.

This isn't just about compatibility; it's about covenant. Being unequally yoked opens spiritual doors. The spirit spouse can take advantage of this frustration, presenting a counterfeit partner who seems perfect, except for the most important thing which is their walk with God. When you settle for a partner outside the faith, you're also unknowingly agreeing with a spirit of compromise. That compromise weakens your spiritual covering, and the warfare that follows is intense.

It is better to wait and obey than to marry in haste and fight unnecessary battles. Your spouse should not be your mission field. The one you marry should be someone who walks with Christ and can war with you, not against you. The spirit spouse thrives in places where God's order has been ignored to destroy marriages.

2. Disposable Marriage

In today's society, the concept of marriage has drastically shifted. Once revered as a sacred institution meant to be cherished and preserved for life, marriage is now increasingly viewed as a temporary arrangement, something to be discarded when it no longer serves its purpose. In a world where instant gratification often trumps long-term commitment, the idea of staying in a marriage "for better or for worse" seems outdated to many. The rise of temporary unions, such as contractual marriages, casual partnerships, or relationships based solely on convenience, has contributed to the erosion of the sanctity of marriage.

Spirit spouses thrive in this environment of detachment and instability. The spiritual forces that work to disrupt marriages find fertile ground in relationships that are entered into with a transient mindset. When individuals marry without the intention of enduring the highs and lows, the challenges, and the emotional work required to nurture a lasting union, they inadvertently open themselves up to spiritual manipulation. These forces exploit their insecurities, doubts, and lack of commitment, fostering mistrust, emotional distance, and a gradual loss of intimacy.

To combat this, couples must return to the understanding that marriage is a sacred covenant, a bond meant to be nurtured, protected, and valued. A shift in mindset is necessary, moving away from the idea of marriage as disposable and toward one of enduring commitment. By rejecting the influence of spirit spouses and embracing the hard work, patience, and sacrifice that come with a lasting partnership, couples can rediscover the strength and beauty of marriage.

3. Unprepared for Forever

The wedding, often viewed as the pinnacle of the couple's relationship, has become more of an occasion for societal approval than a personal milestone for the partners involved. There's no shortage of pressure to create the perfect wedding day, an event that meets the expectations of friends, family, and the broader community. Couples spend months or even years planning every detail of the wedding, from the venue to the attire, the decorations, and the guest list. Yet, too often, they neglect to invest the same level of thought and effort into preparing for the marriage itself. **Where money could have been spent on personal and joint therapy sessions for the couple to heal, and time spent and money sown into a deliverance minister to cast out ancestral demons, the celebration of the wedding day becomes the focus, while the long-term commitment and work of marriage are left largely unexplored.**

Spirit spouses take advantage of the lack of preparation, particularly in marriages where couples fail to understand the depth of the commitment they've made. When individuals aren't armed with the tools to deal with the challenges of marriage, emotional vulnerability becomes an opening for spiritual interference.

However, couples who invest in their marriage early on by seeking deliverance, attending relationship seminars, and engaging in counseling build a strong spiritual and emotional foundation that protects their relationship. They are more resilient in the face of challenges, better equipped to confront conflicts, and far more likely to experience lasting love. These couples have the tools to resist the pressures that spirit spouses and other destructive forces bring to bear on their union.

4. Shifting Roles: A Breeding Ground for Conflict

Traditional gender roles in marriage, where men provided and protected and women nurtured, have become blurred in to-day's shifting cultural and professional landscape. This has left many couples confused and frustrated, with each partner uncertain about their role. Wives may feel pressured to over-compensate, while husbands may feel emasculated or unsure of their place.

This role confusion often leads to emotional distance and un-resolved conflict, creating an environment where spirit spouses thrive. These spiritual forces exploit insecurity, re-sentment, and unmet expectations, whispering lies that deepen division and foster mistrust. What starts as minor disagree-ments can escalate into major emotional wounds.

Modern narratives, like "anything a man can do, a woman can do better," while empowering, can unintentionally create competition in marriage instead of partnership. As both spouses try to prove their worth, tension grows, and emotional intimacy fades. The key to overcoming this is recognizing that roles in marriage don't have to be rigid. A thriving marriage is built on balance, mutual respect, and spiritual unity, not on outdated cultural expectations. Spirit spouses lose their influence when couples stand together in clarity, humility, and love.

5. The Brokenness of Emotional Distance

This was something I personally experienced in my marriage. Emotional distance, fueled by unresolved conflict and lack of vulnerability, created a breeding ground for the enemy. My husband and I had recurring arguments, especially when I was sick. I expected him to stay home and help with the kids, knowing he had unused sick days. But I never asked directly. I feared seeming weak. So, I stayed silent, then lashed out later, "You don't love me." He, feeling attacked, defended himself, "I have to work!" Then came the silence, days without speaking. And during those silent nights, the tormenting spirit spouse returned.

I cried out to God. In prayer, He revealed a deeper cycle: the argument wasn't just causing the spiritual attacks; it was part of the trap. The spirit spouse exploited a wound in me from childhood: fear of being seen as weak, rejected, and controlled. God showed me that healing required me to stop focusing on my husband's behavior and ask, "What's my wound in this argument?" As I fasted and prayed, God brought me back to my teenage years and exposed the lie I believed. He replaced it with His truth, and I began to heal.

Eventually, the same situation arose, but this time I responded differently. I calmly said, "Honey, I don't feel well. Could you take a day off to help with the kids?" At first, he reacted angrily and left. But I stayed calm, healed, and grounded. Ten minutes later, he returned, apologized, and we talked. I asked gently, "Why don't you ever take time off?" He opened up about his financial anxiety. That conversation opened the door for emotional vulnerability in our marriage. We began a healing journey together, exposing wounds, praying, and inviting God into our broken places.

Healing starts with us. We can't fix our spouse, but we can invite God to heal our wounds, change our responses, and break the cycle the enemy wants to keep going. Emotional vulnerability disarms the spirit spouse and invites intimacy. When we allow God to heal us, we create space for our marriage to thrive.

How to Fight and Win Like a Christian in Marriage

Every marriage will inevitably face conflict. It's not a matter of if disagreements will arise, but when and how you handle them that truly matters. Whether it's a small misunderstanding or a deep, ongoing issue, conflict is a natural part of any relationship, especially one as intimate as marriage. After all, you are two distinct individuals, each shaped by different experiences, backgrounds, and personalities.

But here's the key: how you approach conflict is what defines the strength of your marriage. Conflict doesn't have to be destructive; it can be an opportunity to grow stronger as a couple, to build deeper understanding, and to draw closer together. Unfortunately, many couples view conflict as an obstacle or something to be avoided at all costs, but the truth is, conflict can actually become one of your most powerful tools for building a lasting, resilient marriage. When conflict arises, it's crucial to remember that your goal isn't to win the argument or prove who's right. The true goal is to win together, to come out on the other side with a deeper appreciation for one another and a renewed commitment to the relationship. Let us explore how to approach conflict in a way that honors God, builds your marriage, and helps you fight and win together. With the right perspective and tools, you can turn the inevitable struggles into steppingstones toward a stronger, more loving relationship.

The Power of Communication: Protecting Your Marriage from Spirit Spouses

Effective communication is the lifeline of a healthy marriage and a strong defense against spirit spouses because they thrive on emotional distance, confusion, and poor communication. When couples don't talk openly, these entities exploit the silence, planting lies that breed mistrust and isolation.

My husband and I overcame their influence by adopting a "check-in" practice. He regularly asked, "How am I doing as a husband?" Though it was hard at first, it eventually led to honest conversations and even couples therapy, which brought deep healing. Now, we both make open communication a priority. We also pray before difficult conversations, asking God for boldness, compassion, and protection against spiritual interference. This intentionality has strengthened our connection and shut the door to the enemy. We apply the same approach with our children, teaching them to express their feelings freely so spirit spouses can't exploit emotional confusion.

Good communication doesn't happen by chance; it takes practice, prayer, and humility. But it's one of the most powerful tools to guard your marriage and family from spiritual attack.

Talking: Speaking with Clarity and Intentionality

Many couples struggle with truly effective communication, often falling into the trap of talking at each other rather than talking to each other. This subtle difference is far more important than it might seem. An essential part of effective communication in marriage is being open to the idea of listening. Spirit spouses thrive on misunderstandings and emotional detachment, and listening carefully to your partner is one of the most powerful ways to combat that. Active listening means being fully present, setting aside distractions, and giving your spouse the attention they deserve. It's not just about hearing the words; it is about understanding the deeper emotions and needs behind those words. When you make your spouse feel truly heard, you build trust and understanding, making it much harder for spiritual forces to create division.

Probing questions open the door to vulnerable conversations that allow both partners to reflect on their emotional and spiritual needs. Spirit spouses often take advantage of couples who don't engage in these deeper conversations. They thrive in an environment where partners assume they already know everything about each other or where they shy away from discussing difficult feelings. But when you ask questions that invite your partner to share their inner thoughts and experiences, you build intimacy, trust, and connection that spiritual forces can't easily infiltrate.

Some questions can be simple yet profound, like:

- ❖ "What do you think about where we are in our marriage right now? Do you feel we're growing together or drifting apart?"
- ❖ "Has this marriage brought joy and fulfillment to your life in the ways you hoped it would?"
- ❖ "What are some things you've learned about yourself since we've been married?"
- ❖ "Do you ever feel like I'm not seeing or hearing you for who you truly are?"
- ❖ "Is there anything about our relationship that makes you feel misunderstood or neglected?"
- ❖ "Are there areas in our marriage where you feel we're not fully aligned with God's will?"
- ❖ "What's one thing that's been weighing on you that we haven't had a chance to talk about yet?"
- ❖ "Do you feel there's any emotional distance between us that we need to address?"
- ❖ "What are some things I could do to make you feel more supported or loved?"

The Importance of Creating a Safe Space

For these conversations to be truly effective, it's crucial that both partners feel safe to share without fear of judgment, anger, or retaliation. Communication must occur in an environment of emotional safety where both people can express their thoughts and feelings freely. Spirit spouses thrive on fear and control, so it's important that you and your partner work to create an atmosphere of love and trust.

To truly listen, you must be willing to suspend judgment and put aside your own emotional needs for a moment. Instead of jumping to conclusions or rushing to give advice, take a step back and absorb what your partner is saying. Try to understand their emotions, their body language, and the deeper feelings that might not be immediately apparent. When you listen with this level of attentiveness, you build a connection that spirit spouses cannot easily penetrate.

So, what does active listening look like in practice? It means asking clarifying questions and allowing your spouse to express their feelings fully before responding. Questions like "What do you need from me right now?" or "How can I support you through this?" open the door to deeper understanding. You're not simply listening to respond; you're listening to connect, empathize, and help heal any emotional wounds that may have been caused by previous misunderstandings or frustrations.

Creating a safe space for your spouse to speak freely requires more than just listening. It also involves **emotional intelligence**, the ability to pick up on emotional cues and respond in a way that shows you truly care. Spirit spouses thrive on confusion and misunderstanding, but active listening dismantles their influence by promoting clear, open communication. When both partners feel heard and understood, the foundation of the relationship is strengthened, and spirit spouses are forced to retreat.

Practical Ways to Cultivate Understanding

1. **Ask Questions with Compassionate Curiosity**

   When your spouse seems upset, don't rush to assumptions. Instead, ask yourself, what's really going on in their heart? What emotions might they be struggling to express? Approach them with genuine curiosity, not to interrogate but to understand. A simple question like, "How are you feeling today?" can open the door to meaningful conversations.

2. **Validate Their Emotions**

   Even if your spouse's feelings seem irrational or exaggerated, resist the urge to dismiss them. Instead of saying, "That's not a big deal," try saying, "I can see this really matters to you. Let's work through it together." This kind of response shows respect for their emotional experience and strengthens your connection.

3. **Navigate Emotional Triggers with Care**

   Every person has emotional triggers and sensitive areas that can cause strong reactions. Understanding these triggers in your spouse and approaching them with care can prevent unnecessary conflict. Instead of reacting defensively, take a moment to breathe and respond with empathy.

4. **Research Your Partner's Childhood**

   Talk to your partner or trusted family members and friends who knew your partner in their formative years. Listen with curiosity when stories of your partner's childhood are told, looking to uncover wounded places that you can help heal. This will enable you to understand some of their protective mechanisms and help them pull down the walls that keep you both apart. When both partners actively pursue understanding, the walls that spirit spouses seek to exploit crumble. Empathy, validation, and humility act as spiritual armor, protecting your marriage from division. Spirit spouses cannot thrive in an environment of love and connection, where misunderstandings are addressed with compassion and conflicts are resolved with grace.

5. **Feedback: Responding with Love and Constructive Solutions**

More than just critique, feedback, when shared with love and respect, is an opportunity for growth, deeper connection, and emotional intimacy. The tone, timing, and intent matter. Loving feedback invites unity, harsh or absent feedback breeds resentment and silence. Consistent, compassionate feedback acts as a spiritual shield. It should be a regular practice, not just used in a crisis. When couples celebrate wins, address concerns gently, and stay emotionally engaged, they create a bond that spirit spouses can't easily infiltrate. If communication has already been broken? Begin with prayer, even if your spouse isn't ready to engage. God can begin healing in the hearts of those willing to act in faith.

Sample Prayer

- In the name of Jesus, I bind you, spirit spouse, and cast you out of the communication lines between me and my spouse. I command you to open all closed portals of communication that you have previously closed, now in Jesus' name. I speak Isaiah 60:11 over my spouse's and my communication, and I declare that the gates are open for me and my spouse to communicate with love and understanding.

- I cast out of my marriage and terminate the assignment of every demonic spirit on assignment to afflict my marriage with the "Tower of Babel syndrome," causing me and my husband to speak different languages to each other, which we cannot understand. (Genesis 11:1-9).

- I pray, heavenly Father, that today, You will give my spouse an insatiable desire, which will last all through our marriage, to want to communicate with me deeply and honestly in a loving and nonjudgmental manner. All this I pray in Jesus' name Amen

6. Take Control of Anger Before It Controls You

Anger is a powerful and natural emotion, but it's also one of the most explosive emotions we experience in marriage. The Bible acknowledges that it's okay to feel anger but provides a clear warning: "In your anger do not sin" (Ephesians 4:26). Anger is like fire; it can warm your heart and your home or burn everything to the ground. When controlled and directed properly, anger can help bring unresolved issues to light, allowing for resolution and growth. But when left unchecked, anger can build a wall between you and your spouse, causing long-lasting damage and emotional distance.

Spirit spouses thrive in environments where anger is allowed to fester. They don't need much to work with, just a spark of irritation or frustration. They can take a minor disagreement, twist it, and turn it into a fiery argument that consumes both partners. They whisper lies into your heart, fueling bitterness and making it nearly impossible to reconcile. The spirit spouse tells you, "You don't deserve this," "They don't care about you," and "This will never change." It makes you feel isolated, misunderstood, and emotionally disconnected from your spouse. But anger is not the enemy; how we handle it is what matters.

The Bible teaches us that anger is a signal, not a weapon. It's an emotional response that highlights deeper issues, unmet needs, or unresolved hurt. Instead of letting it control us, we are called to pause and reflect. The apostle James reminds us, "Everyone should be quick to listen, slow to speak, and slow to become angry, because human anger does not produce the righteousness that God desires" (James 1:19-20). Anger, when harnessed with wisdom, can reveal the root of the issue and provide an opportunity for healing.

When a disagreement arises, don't let anger escalate into a battle. Rather than attacking your spouse with harsh words, take a step back. Pause and pray for clarity. Ask God for the wisdom to see beyond the surface issue and understand the deeper emotions that are driving your frustration. Instead of responding with defensiveness or harshness, choose to redirect your anger toward resolution and reconciliation. It may feel like a battle at the moment, but when you fight with love and understanding, you disarm the enemy, both the emotional pain and the spirit spouse that seeks to cause division.

7. **Address Issues Quickly**

Don't let resentment take root. Unresolved conflict is like a ticking time bomb in your marriage, quietly building, ready to explode at the worst moment. The longer you let issues go unaddressed, the more damage they can cause, not just to your relationship but to your emotional and spiritual health. What might start as a small misunderstanding can, over time, grow into a mountain of resentment, bitterness, and emotional distance. But here's the thing: when left unchecked, the enemy, especially spirit spouses, find ways to creep into that silence, using your unresolved issues to plant seeds of doubt, anger, and separation.

Ephesians 4:26 reminds us, "In your anger, do not sin. Do not let the sun go down while you are still angry." It's not just about managing anger but about handling it quickly before it turns into something bigger. You're not called to resolve every conflict in an instant, but you are called to address it. If you let the sun go down on your anger, it doesn't just affect you; it opens the door to bitterness and spiritual forces, like spirit spouses, who thrive in the darkness of unresolved issues. These entities whisper to you. "He doesn't care," "She'll never change," and "This marriage is doomed." They use your pain as an entry point, pushing you further apart. But what if, instead of letting anger grow into resentment, you took a moment to pause, to reflect, and to address the problem? When you confront issues early and clearly, you create space for resolution, for healing, and for peace. The longer you wait, the more damage is done, not just to your emotional well-being but to your spiritual health.

8. **Overcome Pride**

Admit When You're Wrong. Pride is the silent destroyer in relationships, often going unnoticed until it has already caused irreparable damage. It whispers in your ear, "You're right, and they are wrong." It convinces you that your perspective is the only valid one, and any acknowledgment of your mistakes would mean you're weak or less worthy. But pride doesn't resolve conflicts; it only deepens them. Spirit spouses know exactly how to exploit pride. When pride enters the picture, it acts as a barrier to true connection. It feeds the lie that you are right, even when you know deep down that your actions or words may have hurt your spouse. It convinces you that admitting your faults would be a weakness when, in reality, it is the most powerful thing you can do to restore peace. The longer pride reigns in your heart, the more you allow these spiritual forces to create a rift between you and your partner.

Humility, then, is the antidote to pride. It doesn't mean you're always at fault or that your feelings don't matter. It simply means that you are willing to see the situation from your spouse's perspective and recognize your role in the conflict. Humility means saying, "I'm sorry," without the need to justify your actions or deflect blame. It's about owning your part in the argument and taking responsibility for how you contributed to the problem. In doing so, you create a safe space for your spouse to do the same, fostering an environment where love and grace can flourish.

9. **Forgive and Let Go**

Forgiveness is more than just a choice. It is a powerful spiritual weapon, one that can break chains and unlock healing in your marriage. It's often misunderstood as excusing the hurt or pretending it didn't happen, but that's not what forgiveness is. It's a deliberate decision to release the grip of bitterness, resentment, and anger, even when the other person may not deserve it. It's about choosing love over hate, peace over conflict, and healing over brokenness.

In Colossians 3:13, the Bible teaches us, "Forgive as the Lord forgave you." This is the ultimate example of grace. God's forgiveness isn't conditional; it's unconditional. He forgave us when we were undeserving, when we had no way of repaying Him. And as His followers, we are called to reflect that same forgiveness in our relationships. It's not about whether or not the other person "deserves" it, but about what forgiveness does for you and your marriage.

Spirit spouses whisper lies in the midst of unforgiveness, telling you things like "They don't deserve your forgiveness," "You'll never heal from this," or "This will always be a part of your relationship." These lies prevent healing, make reconciliation difficult, and slowly build walls of emotional distance between you and your spouse. The more you allow those thoughts to take root, the more you give these spiritual forces the power to stop you and your spouse from accomplishing the divine and beautiful purpose for which God put you together. But forgiveness acts as a spiritual shield, disarming the power of the enemy and stopping spirit spouses from wreaking havoc in your marriage. When you choose to forgive, you starve these negative forces. You shut the door on their influence and invite peace, restoration, and healing into your relationship. Forgiveness breaks the chains of anger, resentment, and bitterness, and it clears the way for both of you to move forward together in unity and love.

How to Forgive

So, how do you forgive when the hurt feels unbearable? You start with your will. The first step toward forgiveness happens when you decide you want to forgive. God honors this first step, and he will be moved to help you. Next, pray for strength and guidance. Ask God to help you release the pain and bitterness. Remember that forgiveness is a process, not a one-time event. You choose it daily, even when the wounds are fresh. When you struggle to forgive, ask God to give you the heart of Christ, who forgave us all, even when we were undeserving.

Sample forgiveness prayer

Dear heavenly Father, I come to you to declare that I choose to forgive (insert name) for (insert what was done to you).

Please help me by the power of Your Holy Spirit to forgive (insert name).

Please take me to the place where my emotions match my will.

I release (insert name) and declare that they owe me nothing but love. I release all bitterness and offense for what (insert name) did to me, and I let them go and send them the love of Jesus. I understand that even if they tried, they could never heal me where they hurt me. Heavenly Father, You are the only one who can heal me where I am hurting because of what (insert name) did to me. Please heal me, Lord, take away my pain, and comfort my heart as only you can. All this I pray in Jesus' name. Amen.

Guarding Your Heart in Marriage

Every marriage, no matter how strong, faces moments of temptation, often in the form of what might seem like innocent emotions. Affection for someone other than your spouse doesn't typically appear as a full-blown affair right from the start. It creeps in, almost unnoticed, through friendly conversation, a lingering compliment, or an unexpected connection with someone outside the relationship. At first, it might seem harmless, even flattering. However, when we allow these small sparks of affection to go unchecked, they can quickly grow into something more dangerous, leading us down a path of temptation and, ultimately, sin.

The real test is in how we handle those feelings. It's not about denying that attraction might arise; it's about making a conscious, intentional choice to redirect that affection back to the one we've committed ourselves to. We must remember in such times that our commitment to our spouse is supposed to mirror our commitment to Christ, who is our legal, spiritual spouse. The marriage relationship here on earth is supposed to represent Christ's relationship with His bride, the church (Ephesians 5:25, Revelations 21:9). Our spouse is the one we have chosen, the one we've vowed to love, honor, and cherish. That commitment should be the compass that guides all of our emotions, especially the ones that might otherwise lead us astray.

How to Cope with Extramarital Attraction

The first step to handling extramarital attraction is to acknowledge it. Don't pretend it's not happening or brush it off as something that will just go away. Ignoring the feelings can lead to a slow burn of dissatisfaction, resentment, and temptation. The key is to address it immediately. When you sense your attention shifting away from your spouse, stop. Take a moment to evaluate what's happening internally. What's driving this emotional pull? Is there an area in your marriage that needs attention, communication, emotional intimacy, or physical affection that you're trying to find elsewhere?

Attraction doesn't just pop up without reason. Often, it's a symptom of something deeper: an unmet need, a desire for connection, or an emotional disconnect. Once you identify the root cause of your feelings, don't shy away from addressing it. This isn't about shaming yourself for experiencing attraction; it's about being proactive in protecting the sanctity of your marriage.

Next, take the issue to God in prayer. Start by repenting for any past generational sin of adultery on behalf of yourself and your spouse and cast out any demons that may have taken advantage of this sin to ensure that you find yourself in this position. Next, sit with God and ask the Holy Spirit to help you identify the wound in your relationship with your spouse, which is at the root of the attraction you feel toward another person. Invite him to show you the unmet need. Next, take action. Have a conversation about your unmet need with your spouse. Don't hide your feelings, but instead, approach them with honesty and vulnerability. Maybe you're struggling with communication, or there's a lack of intimacy that's causing emotional distance between you. Sit down together, without the distractions of daily life, and have an open conversation about how you're feeling. You don't have to solve everything in one conversation, but the act of addressing the problem will break down barriers and help you reconnect and take away those feelings of attraction.

But what if the problem isn't something that can be solved in a single conversation? Take steps to nurture your relationship over time. Seek counseling, find new ways to bond with each other, or simply commit to spending more intentional time together. When you redirect that emotional energy back to your spouse, you not only strengthen the bond you have but also build resilience against outside temptations.

Spirit spouses know when there is a crack in the armor of your marriage, and they exploit it. They thrive when you feel lonely, bored, or disconnected in your marriage. This is why it is very important for couples to have a shared burning purpose they can engage in together. The more you redirect your affection and attention back to your spouse, the more you shut the door on the spirit's spouse's influence. It's like cutting off their power source. The more intentional and engaged you are in your marriage, the harder it becomes for these forces to pull you away.

Dealing with the Sin of Adultery

Adultery is a serious breach of trust, a sin that cuts to the core of a marriage and leaves lasting scars. Yet, while it is a grievous act, it is not an unforgivable one. If you find yourself caught in the web of temptation or have already crossed that line, don't allow shame to isolate you. The road to healing begins with truth, and the first step is confession, being brutally honest with yourself and with your spouse. It's easy to hide, bury the shame, and try to cover up your actions, but this will only prolong the pain. Facing the truth head-on is where freedom begins. Admitting your wrongdoing is not just about confessing to your spouse; it's about acknowledging that you have broken God's heart, too.

Moving Forward: The Path to Healing

For the one who committed infidelity, consistency is key. Your partner needs time to see that your promises are real. Be patient with their lack of trust. It will take repeated actions of integrity to rebuild what was broken. Apologies alone aren't enough. You must ask yourself, *Why did this happen?* What inner wound were you trying to numb? Healing requires deep self-reflection and often professional help. Without this, the cycle may repeat.

For the one betrayed, the road is painful. God understands it's why He permits divorce in cases of infidelity (Matthew 5:32). But if you choose to stay, you must also choose to forgive. Don't stay if you plan to hold the offense over your spouse forever. Forgiveness doesn't mean forgetting, but it does mean letting go. Only then can healing begin (Matthew 6:14).

Rebuilding intimacy is a joint effort. If you've been hurt, open your heart slowly and trust God first. Tell Him you're trusting your spouse in honor of Him and surrender the outcome to His care. Pour out your pain to God, ask Him to soften your heart, remove obsessive thoughts, and rekindle love between you and your spouse. Seek God's wisdom at every step. He promises to guide you (Proverbs 2:6) and to be near the brokenhearted (Psalms 34:18). Let His peace lead you.

Sex within Marriage: A Powerful Weapon against the Spirit Spouse

Sexual intimacy is one of the most profound ways a couple can connect, yet far too often, it becomes a battleground for selfish desires or a mechanical act to fulfill duty rather than a shared, intimate experience. When one partner's pleasure is prioritized over the other's, or when intimacy becomes an act of duty, it can create emotional gaps that grow over time. These gaps are fertile ground for spirit spouses to take root.

My Story: The Power of Orgasmic Pleasure against the Spirit Spouse

Take, for example, what happened in my own marriage. At the time, I was operating from a shame-based view of sexuality. I treated sex like a chore, something to check off the list, like doing laundry or washing dishes. I approached intimacy with a sense of obligation rather than joy. I didn't allow my husband to explore my body or focus on areas like my clitoris that were designed to bring pleasure and connection. Orgasm felt unreachable. It wasn't even something I expected, let alone embraced.

While I struggled to connect with my husband, I was consistently experiencing orgasms in my dreams. Demonic entities would visit me in the night, and I would wake up either mid-orgasm or with a heavy, dark presence hovering over me as my body responded on its own. The moments were physically intense, sometimes even pleasurable for a few seconds, but they always left me spiritually wrecked. I'd be bedbound for hours, sometimes days, unable to function until I cried out in warfare prayer.

These spiritual attacks weren't random. They were strategic. Every time I had something important coming like an interview, a personal goal, or a breakthrough, I would experience one of these unholy encounters, and I just knew that door would slam shut. So I ran to my secret place. I cried out to God with everything in me. In the stillness of prayer, I heard Him speak:

"Why do you refuse to have orgasms with your husband?"

It stopped me in my tracks. God was confronting me, but in the most loving, liberating way. He was inviting me to trust Him with my sexuality, to see it not as something dirty or disconnected from my faith, but as something sacred. Slowly, He gave me the courage to trust my husband too. To let go of fear. To start talking. God, in His kindness, began to teach me. He led me to research the female orgasm, its design, and the beauty of pleasure within the covenant. He reminded me, **"I created sex. I created pleasure. I created you."** And then He brought me to Revelation 4:11:

"You are worthy, our Lord and God, to receive glory and honor and power, for you created all things, and by your will they were created and have their being."

The revelation of that Scripture undid me. I had never associated my orgasm with God's pleasure. But He showed me that when I treated sex like a duty and refused to receive the joy He designed for me, I was robbing Him of the glory. I had unknowingly been giving that pleasure to the demonic spirit spouse instead. I began to repent for myself and for the generations before me who embraced a shame-based sexuality. I confessed how I had kept God out of that part of my life, as if He wasn't holy enough to touch it. God said to me, "How can you call your sexuality dirty when I created it? Let me in. I will cleanse it. I will heal it. And we will enjoy it together." That was a radical shift for me. God wanted to be a part of my sexuality. Even mine. Even after everything. I was created for His pleasure. And that pleasure included intimacy within marriage. I had finally found the way out.

I started to worship with my body through intimacy with my husband. I let go of shame. I invited my husband, who had waited so patiently, to lead me in love. I opened myself up to receive pleasure as a gift from God, not a weapon from the enemy. Our intimacy transformed. We began to laugh, talk, and explore together. Orgasm became not just a possibility, but an act of worship. The spirit spouse was locked out. My gates were no longer open to darkness but fully open to Jesus, the King of Glory. He came in, and everything changed. Hallelujah.

Sex in Marriage as an Act of Worship

Sex in marriage is not simply about the physical oneness between husband and wife; it's a powerful and symbolic reflection of the deep and eternal relationship that Christ shares with His bride, the Church. This isn't just a casual metaphor; it is a divine truth meant to shape the way we view sexual intimacy in marriage.

This act of unashamed offering of our body to our spouse mirrors the way we should offer ourselves as living sacrifices to God, holy, surrendered, and pure. Just as Genesis 2:25 tells us, "Adam and his wife were both naked, and they felt no shame." Intimacy in marriage was designed to be an act of vulnerability and trust, free from shame and fear. This unashamed, selfless giving in marriage reflects the heart of Christ's love for His Church, a love that is unconditional, sacrificial, and redemptive.

When we engage in sexual intimacy with our spouse, it becomes an offering of love, an act of worship that honors God's design for marriage. Every touch, every embrace, and every shared moment of closeness is an opportunity to worship through the physical union that mirrors the spiritual union between Christ and His Church.

Understanding the Female and Male Anatomy: Honoring Each Other's Needs

A thriving sexual relationship is one where both partners feel loved, respected, and truly seen. Yet, for many couples, there is a lack of understanding or communication when it comes to their own bodies and the intricate ways their bodies respond to touch and affection. This misunderstanding creates a disconnect, and over time, this emotional gap can open a door for destructive forces, like spirit spouses, to thrive. However, a deeper understanding of both the male and female anatomy can help combat these forces, build a more intimate connection, and ultimately protect the marriage from these spiritual attacks.

The Female Anatomy: Understanding Her Needs

In many marriages, the physical and emotional complexities of the female body remain largely unexplored by many men. One area that is particularly misunderstood or even neglected is the clitoris. This small yet powerful organ is crucial for female sexual pleasure, containing a dense network of nerve endings that, when properly stimulated, can lead to intense pleasure, intimacy, and orgasm. Yet, despite its significance, many men focus primarily on penetration, often overlooking the fact that a woman's sexual fulfillment is not solely dependent on this physical act.

The reality is that for most women, sexual satisfaction is deeply intertwined with emotional connection. For a woman to truly feel fulfilled, she needs more than just physical intimacy; she needs to feel seen, heard, and emotionally secure in her relationship. The clitoris is an important part of this dynamic. Its stimulation is not just about pleasure; it is about connection, respect, and the act of caring for her needs. When men neglect this aspect of intimacy, it can cause emotional disconnection. Over time, this emotional distance breeds frustration, loneliness, and unmet desires. In these moments, where emotional intimacy falters, spirit spouses often find an opening. They may whisper lies into the minds of both partners. For the wife, these lies might sound like "You're not being seen," "Your needs don't matter," or "You deserve more than this." As the wife feels more disconnected and unfulfilled, she may start to seek validation and comfort from other sources, emotionally or even physically, leading her away from the marriage.

But when a husband takes the time to understand the female body, particularly the clitoris, and prioritizes his wife's pleasure, he begins to break down these walls of emotional distance. This was the path to much of my sexual healing. My husband took the time early on in our marriage to establish the fact that he was more concerned about my sexual fulfillment than his own.

Every woman is unique, and to truly connect with her on a deeper level, a husband must be attuned to her desires, preferences, and emotional needs. The key to fulfilling intimacy is to approach foreplay with patience, taking the time to learn and appreciate the subtle ways in which his wife responds. Whether it's the way she reacts to his touch, the sounds she makes when she's content, or the way she expresses herself emotionally, understanding these cues is critical for creating a satisfying experience for both partners.

The husband should understand that when he chooses the path of focusing on his wife's sexual and emotional needs, he creates a deeper sense of connection and intimacy within the marriage, which he will enjoy. Moreover, this investment in the physical and emotional aspects of marriage creates a buffer against spirit spouses. When both partners engage in a deep, loving, and intentional sexual connection, spirit spouses cannot thrive in that environment.

The Male Anatomy: Understanding His Needs While understanding female anatomy is crucial, women must also take the time to understand the male body and the unique ways it responds to touch. Though the male body may seem simpler in structure, it is still complex in its needs and reactions.

The penis and testicles are key areas of sexual pleasure, but equally important is the emotional connection a man experiences during intimacy. For many men, feeling desired, respected, and emotionally connected to their wives is just as vital as the physical act of sex itself. When a man feels appreciated, his sexual experience is heightened. But when his emotional needs, especially for respect, are neglected, he can begin to feel isolated or rejected, opening a door for spirit spouses to influence the marriage.

Wives should also keep in mind that men are highly visual when it comes to sexual arousal. Investing in the way your body looks is not vanity; it's intimacy. Maintain a healthy diet and exercise, not just for your well-being, but also to stay attractive to your husband. Walk around naked sometimes; to him, this is foreplay. Wear the clothes he likes and choose hairstyles that he finds sexually appealing. For example, one of the key reasons I wear my hair in locs is because my husband finds them incredibly attractive. I am intentional about it because I know it blesses our connection.

Feeding your man is another powerful form of foreplay. Yes, feeding him good food, especially something you've made with care, is sexually stimulating. If you don't know how to cook, maybe you can learn how to bake. At the very least, have one special meal you've mastered or order something he enjoys to eat and serve it to him in a special way. There is something deeply intimate and bonding about nourishing your man with food, and it ties directly into his sense of being cared for, honored, and desired.

Above all, initiate sex as often as you can. Men long to feel wanted, not just needed. When a wife takes the lead in initiating intimacy, it reassures her husband of her desire and love for him. This act alone can heal emotional wounds, dismantle pride, and deepen connection. By initiating, you communicate to him that you are not just available, but eager and engaged, and this is powerful.

And wives, don't be silent during sex. Be vocal, curious, and engaged. Explore your husband's body. Ask what he enjoys.

Show interest. This openness builds a safe space for deep connection and pleasure, and it tells your husband that you are not just participating, but that you're present, enthusiastic, and if something feels good, whether it's a gentle touch, a loving word, or a shared gaze, feel free to express it. Verbalizing what you enjoy or simply communicating your feelings allows your husband to understand you better and respond more lovingly. During sexual intimacy, the act of expressing pleasure or discomfort with kindness builds a rhythm between you and your husband. In Song of Solomon 1:2, the bride is not ashamed to declare a heartfelt plea, "Let him kiss me with the kisses of his mouth, for your love is more delightful than wine."

As women, we sometimes carry the weight of past experiences or insecurities that can hinder our ability to be fully present during intimacy. However, when we allow ourselves to embrace the moment with joy, we open the door for a deeper connection with our spouse. This doesn't mean that there won't be challenges or moments of discomfort, but when we communicate openly and lovingly, those challenges can be navigated together. The beauty of intimacy lies in the shared vulnerability and the willingness to learn and grow together.

When Orgasm Feels Like an Unreachable Dream

Ladies let's be honest, orgasm is often painted as the ultimate destination of sexual intimacy, but for many women, reaching it feels more like a myth than reality. Studies suggest that 30–40% of women struggle with climax, and some quietly admit they're not even sure if they've ever experienced one. The frustration this causes can create an emotional distance that goes unnoticed at first but grows over time. To "keep the peace," many women resort to faking it, an act that may seem harmless at the moment, but deep down, it's not the solution. Instead, it adds another layer of disconnection between husband and wife and can become an open door for spirit spouse dream-induced orgasms, which can birth financial struggles and strange infirmities, etc. I challenge you, women, to open up about this to God and then to your husband so you both can begin the process of reclaiming this powerful part of your intimacy.

So, what's the root cause of this challenge? The reasons vary, but one of the most common is inadequate foreplay for women. Men who have struggled with porn addiction and masturbation may also struggle to attain orgasm with their wives, as they may be unable to enjoy a slower, more deliberate, and less stimulating sexual environment with their wives. Men, be patient with yourself as you partner with God, and he detoxifies your sexuality and teaches you how to enjoy sex within the confines of marriage. Don't be afraid to ask a trusted brother in Christ to help you pray to overcome.

Premature Ejaculation: A Call for Vulnerability

Premature ejaculation is one of the most misunderstood challenges in marriage. It can also be a symptom of spirit spouse oppression for men. For a man, it can feel like a loss of identity or masculinity, triggering feelings of shame, frustration, and fear. For a woman, it may spark doubts about her attractiveness or her husband's love. But premature ejaculation is not the end of intimacy. It's a challenge that requires understanding, teamwork, and sometimes professional help.

For men, premature ejaculation can feel like a ticking time bomb, a source of stress that threatens to steal the joy of intimacy. It's a common problem, but one that many men struggle to talk about. Why? Because society often ties masculinity to sexual performance, making it hard for men to admit when things don't go as planned. But here's the truth: vulnerability is strength. Husbands, it's okay to share your struggles with your wife. She's your partner, not your critic. When you open up, you give her the chance to support and encourage you rather than silently wondering what went wrong. Husbands and wives should explore techniques that work for both of them, whether it's slowing down, using pauses, or shifting focus. And remember, intimacy isn't just about reaching the finish line; it's about the journey of connection and healing.

Breaking the Cycle: Healing Through Love and Patience.

Healing from intimacy challenges requires more than just surface solutions; it demands a journey of love, patience, and intentional connection. Husbands, this is where your role becomes transformative. If your wife struggles with trust or openness in intimacy, remember that these walls were likely built over years of fear, misunderstanding, and unmet emotional needs. They can't be torn down overnight. What your wife needs most from you is a safe space, a sanctuary where she feels cherished, accepted, and never judged. Talk openly about your own sexual scars and concerns. Invite your wife to your healing journey. Ask her to pray with you and for you when appropriate. Doing this will show her that you are willing to trust her with your scars, and this will create an environment of trust around sexuality within your marriage.

Wives, sharing your story may feel daunting, but it's a step toward freedom. Open up about your fears, doubts, and past experiences. Perhaps you were silenced when you asked questions as a child. Maybe you carry shame or confusion from growing up in an environment where sex was taboo. Your husband isn't just your partner in marriage; he can also be your partner in healing.

The Journey to Freedom

Healing from these wounds is a process, but it's one worth embarking on together. Here are practical steps for couples to move forward:

1. Pray about Sex: Make time to pray about the difficulty you are experiencing sexually in your marriage. Don't shy away from talking to God about the very thing He created. Is He not the best person to show you how to fix it? One thing that helped me in my journey was reading the Song of Solomon over my marriage bed consistently for a season of time. I found that it helped me to get rid of the shame-based sexuality mindset thoughts that had plagued my mind.

2. Reframe Negative Beliefs: Couples who grew up in environments of shame around sex may benefit from reframing those beliefs. This can involve reading books, attending workshops, or seeking counseling to replace those old narratives with healthier ones.

3. Practice Grace and Patience: Healing takes time. Avoid pressuring each other to "fix" things quickly. Instead, focus on celebrating the small steps forward.

4. Seek Professional Help When Needed: Sometimes, the wounds from childhood are too deep to heal on your

own. A professional therapist or counselor can help unpack those experiences, provide tools for better communication, and guide you both toward a healthier, more fulfilling intimacy.

Self-Care: A Couple's Silent Love Language

Cleanliness might not seem like the most exciting aspect of intimacy, but it's undeniably one of the most meaningful. It's an unspoken, yet powerful, expression of love, a way of telling your spouse, "You matter to me, and I care enough to show up at my best for you." Soap, toothpaste, and deodorant are simple, everyday items which might just be the best intimacy aids ever created.

I remember a particularly challenging season in my life when I completely let go of self-care. I stopped doing my hair. I neglected the clothes that once made me feel confident and beautiful. Over time, these small lapses in self-care began to take a toll not just on my sense of self but on my marriage. What started as an internal struggle slowly rippled into the external world. I didn't realize how much my self-neglect was affecting my relationship until I started to notice the subtle changes in my husband's behavior. He seemed distant, unsure, almost as if he didn't recognize the woman he had married. This shift wasn't just a result of one season of neglect; it was a slow fade, one that often happens after the routine of married life sets in.

Women You Know This Is True

During the dating stages, it's easy to keep up the effort. We dress up for dates, wear our best outfits, and put extra care into our appearance. The excitement of being seen and admired by someone new makes us want to present the best version of ourselves. But once the wedding happens and the "honeymoon phase" begins to fade, many of us let go of those habits. We stop investing in our appearance, sometimes without realizing the impact it's having. But it's never too late to make a change. Whether it's taking five extra minutes to shower, putting on a fresh outfit, taking a 30-minute daily walk, or brushing your hair, these small, consistent efforts show your spouse that you're still invested in them and the relationship. It's not about perfection; it's about intentionality. It's about making sure that your spouse feels loved, cared for, and desired.

Men, its Your Turn

Gentlemen, it's time to step up. Cleanliness isn't just a woman's responsibility; it's your responsibility, too. Women have an extraordinary sense of smell. Have you ever noticed your wife walking around, saying, "What's that smell?" while you stand there, completely oblivious? That same sensitivity doesn't disappear when it's time for intimacy. It's not just about the cleanliness of your surroundings; it's about how you show up for her in your marriage.

The Bible calls men to love their wives as themselves, and this applies in every way, including cleanliness. Ephesians 5:28-29 states, "In this same way, husbands ought to love their wives as their own bodies. He who loves his wife loves himself. After all, no one ever hated their own body, but they feed and care for their body, just as Christ does the church." When you look after yourself, you're not just showing respect for your own body, but also for the sacred relationship you share with her. For example, when you make it a habit to take a shower before sex, you are helping to keep your wife free from health issues like urinary tract infections and or yeast infections, which can stem from the bacteria that naturally accumulate on your body throughout the day. A wife who does not have to deal with urinary tract infections or yeast infections after every sexual encounter is more likely to look forward to and enjoy sexual intimacy with you. When you freshen up, when you make yourself attractive not just for the world but for her, it communicates your love and value.

Deliverance in Marriage: A Shared Battle

Some married people remain stuck in their deliverance journey because their spouse has a spirit spouse or is bound by ancestral demonic covenants. If Spouse A undergoes deliverance but Spouse B does not, the spirit spouse from Spouse B can still torment Spouse A through their spiritual union. That's why both spouses must pursue deliverance together. "The two will become one flesh... Whoever is united with the Lord is one with him in spirit" (1 Corinthians 6:16–18).

Here are some signs you may be affected

- ❖ Spouse is uninterested or resistant to prayer/spiritual growth.
- ❖ Spouse is lukewarm, critical, or spiritually disengaged.
- ❖ You experience sexual dreams where the spirit spouse mimics your real spouse.

These symptoms suggest a spiritual crossover: a demonic spirit claiming rights to you through your marital union.

Your response to this should be intercession, not confrontation. You can't nag your spouse into freedom. Instead:

- ❖ Intercede daily for them out of love.
- ❖ Forgive them and fight the real enemy and the spirit behind the behavior.

- ❖ Ask God to lift the veil from their eyes.
- ❖ -Take authority in prayer, using Scripture to cancel the demon's access.
- ❖ -Pray over your marital bed, your spouse's clothing, car, and personal items using anointed oil as a prophetic act of cleansing and sanctification in Jesus' name.

Don't Be Discouraged

If your spouse resists or even turns against you temporarily, know it's the spirit spouse resisting eviction. Keep praying. This may be a season of testing and dying to self, but your persistence in love and humility will break the chain. "Let us not become weary in doing good, for at the proper time we will reap a harvest if we do not give up" (Galatians 6:9). If your spouse begins having tormenting dreams or enters a painful season, it may be God's way of awakening them. When they do come to you, receive them with love and help guide their process, just as God helped you. As you intercede, you close the door of access to the spirit spouse. You don't have to remain bound. Stand in the gap with forgiveness, authority, and unwavering love. In time, God will restore your marriage and turn it into a powerful testimony of deliverance and unity in Christ.

From Foundation to Freedom: A Colorful Covenant Begins

In the chapters leading up to this moment, we've laid the foundation for deliverance. We've uncovered the mystery of the spirit spouse, exposed how it affects our sexuality, and discussed its determined attack against godly marriages. We've walked through truth, building the spiritual awareness needed to stand in victory. Now, it's time to turn our hearts fully toward God's remedy.

The next portion of this book marks a shift from exposure to empowerment. Here, I introduce you to the seven biblical keys that God used to heal and restore me and which brought me consistent victory. Before we dive into these powerful truths, I want to take a moment to talk about something beautiful God did as He gave me each key.

The 7 Color Concepts

When God gave me each of the seven keys, He also revealed a color to go with them. It was as if He was gently washing away the darkness that once clouded my imagination, which was the residue of the spirit spouse, and replacing it with the vibrant light of His truth. I received these colors as my personal rainbow love covenant with God. Just as God gave Noah a sign that the storm was over, I knew in my spirit that this was His promise to me: the covenant with the spirit spouse is broken. It ends with me. I am the generational curse breaker in Jesus' name. I encourage you to meditate on what each color represents and begin to notice these colors in your daily life. Let them become reminders that God's truth is alive around you, speaking to your spirit even through the beauty of nature. Every time your eyes land on one of these colors, let it awaken your spirit to the key it represents.

Pink: Love

A reminder of God's relentless love poured out just for you.

Yellow: Joy

A sign of supernatural joy that is always available to you, no matter the circumstances.

Blue: Worship

A reflection of the sacred space within your soul where you can connect intimately with God.

Red: Grace

A symbol of the abundant grace you've received through Christ's finished work on the cross.

Green: Warfare

A call to spiritual battle. Don't just accept the bad. Some things must be fought through in prayer to change.

Orange: Faith

An invitation to see every situation through the lens of faith rather than fear.

Purple: Freedom

A reminder that you are royalty and free to live as a true son or daughter of the King.

The spirit spouse once hijacked your thoughts and distorted your vision. But now, God is rewiring your mind and refocusing your perspective. He's using the very colors He placed in creation as tools of healing, revelation, and spiritual warfare. From today on, see colors not just as part of creation, but as part of your divine arsenal. Let them speak. Let them remind you. Let them help you win.

THE KEY OF LOVE

Color in: Pink

CHAPTER 5

THE KEY OF LOVE

One day, during my daily devotional time, I was overwhelmed with tears from the heavy burdens of panic attacks, manifesting as heart palpitations and depression, resulting from the tormenting visits of a spirit spouse (incubus). I felt trapped, lost, and weighed down by a deep darkness that seemed unshakable. In the midst of my prayers, I stumbled upon Mark 12:31, which says, "Love your neighbor as yourself." It seemed like any other day of reading the Scriptures, but this verse hit me differently.

Suddenly, I felt a strong conviction from the Holy Spirit. It was as if He whispered directly into my heart, saying, "Sharon, you do not love yourself. You are disobeying my command, and you need to repent. For you have not received my love for you, and so you do not have love in you. How can I use you to pour out pure love to another?" His words pierced me like a sword, and I was brought to my knees, weeping uncontrollably, realizing that I had been neglecting this crucial aspect of God's command.

In that moment of brokenness, I began to repeatedly whisper the words, "I receive your love for me, Jesus." With each repetition, something extraordinary happened. I felt the heaviness that had been suffocating my chest, slowly beginning to lift. The heart palpitations that had plagued me started to subside, and for the first time in what felt like an eternity, I began to feel lighter, as though the chains that had held me in captivity were being broken, one by one. Even though I couldn't fully comprehend the magnitude of what the Holy Spirit was revealing to me at the time, this moment marked the beginning of a profound journey, one of healing, understanding, and deliverance through the key of love. The journey of true inner healing and deliverance from a spirit spouse begins with **receiving God's love**. When it comes to spiritual warfare and deliverance, love often seems like an unlikely weapon. However, the key to overcoming the deep spiritual bondage of a spirit spouse and the trauma they cause is rooted in one simple but profound truth: **God's love is the most powerful force in the universe.**

CONCEPT 1: RECEIVING GOD'S LOVE

Four Key Areas

God, in His boundless grace, has made provisions for us to receive His love in a way that brings deep and lasting healing.

He desires to fill our lives with His love in four key areas, each of which is essential for our healing and wholeness:

1. God loves me as a parent.
2. God loves me as a sibling.
3. God loves me as a friend.
4. God loves me as a spouse.

As I reflect on my journey, I realize that many of the wounds I carried, wounds that gave the spirit spouse a legal right to torment me, were rooted in a deficiency of love in these four areas. But as I began to receive the fullness of God's love, those wounds started to heal. God started to send new kingdom relationships to heal me, and I could literally place them in either one of these four categories.

These four dimensions of love represent the fullness of God's desire to restore and heal us. Many people who have experienced the torment of a spirit spouse are often deficient in one or more of these areas of love. Our earthly relationships, whether with parents, siblings, friends, or romantic partners, often leave us wounded and broken. These wounds create an opening for spirit spouses to enter our lives, as the enemy seeks to exploit the pain and emptiness left by damaged relationships. For example, when we lack the nurturing love of a parent, we may struggle with feelings of rejection and abandonment. The enemy seizes upon these wounds, whispering lies that reinforce our feelings of unworthiness. Similarly, strained relationships with siblings or friends can leave us feeling isolated and disconnected, driving us into counterfeit relationships sponsored by a spirit spouse.

But it doesn't end there. Romantic relationships, especially those filled with trauma, betrayal, or unfulfilled desires, leave us particularly vulnerable to spirit spouses. They capitalize on our longing for intimacy and connection, offering a counterfeit version of love that only leads to further bondage. But here is the good news: God's love is greater **than all of these wounds**. He offers us real love that heals, restores, and brings true freedom.

God's Love as a Parent

God is your original parent. Your earthly parents were used just as a portal to bring you into this world, but you are God's idea. Your parents did not create you; they are just witnessing your existence, just as you, too, are just witnessing theirs. Psalms 139:13-14 states, "For you created my inmost being; you knit me together in my mother's womb." For those who come from homes where they did not receive parental love, meditating on this verse will bring deep inner healing and deliverance as it affirms that you have a true parent in God. Consider Psalms 103:13 as well, which says, "As a father has compassion on his children, so the Lord has compassion on those who fear Him." God watches over us with a parental heart full of tenderness, longing to heal the wounds caused by an absence of parental love in our lives. If you have ever felt abandoned or neglected by an earthly parent, know that God is not like them. He is the perfect Father who decided to create you and who sees your needs and is able to provide for them in abundance.

God's Love as a Sibling

Jesus Himself is referred to as our elder brother in Scripture. Hebrews 2:11 says, "Both the one who makes people holy and those who are made holy are of the same family. So Jesus is not ashamed to call them brothers and sisters." God's love as a sibling is one of companionship and solidarity. Even when human siblings may have caused pain or rivalry, God's love provides the perfect brotherhood and sisterhood where we are never alone or abandoned.

God's Love as a Friend

In John 15:15, Jesus declares, "I no longer call you servants, because a servant does not know his master's business. Instead, I have called you friends." Friendship with God is a beautiful expression of His desire for intimacy with us. Where earthly friends may have failed, betrayed, or abandoned you, God's friendship is loyal, steadfast, and eternal. He walks with us through every storm, providing comfort, guidance, and encouragement.

God's Love as a Spouse

Finally, God's love as a spouse is perhaps the most intimate and profound. Isaiah 54:5 says, "For your Maker is your husband, the Lord Almighty is His name." God desires to fill the void left by broken romantic relationships, offering us a love that is pure, holy, and unwavering. When we understand that we are the bride of Christ, we can begin to walk in the revelation of the fact that no spirit spouse can have dominion over us. This revelation also gives us the power not to settle for toxic romantic relationships.

Experiencing God's Love Tangibly: The Power of Vulnerability and Relationships

To tangibly experience God's love, the first step is to open ourselves to vulnerability. Vulnerability can seem like the last thing we want to embrace when we've been hurt. However, it's only through vulnerability that healing can begin. We must first allow ourselves to be vulnerable with God, letting Him into the deepest and most broken places of our hearts.

God often uses relationships to bring His love to life in ways that we can feel and see. After we've opened ourselves up to Him, we must also be willing to step out in faith and build connections with people who reflect His love. These relationships, though imperfect, are vehicles for God's grace, healing, and restoration.

Even as we open our hearts to new relationships, we must be careful not to make people into who we want them to be before we've truly seen who they are. Spirit spouses can pressure us to move too fast, trying to fill emotional gaps with the wrong people. God knows what kind of love we need, whether it be fatherly, brotherly, friendly, or romantic. He sends it through the right people at the right time. Watch first. Let people show you who they are before deciding who they are to you.

Stepping into these relationships requires trust and making time to deliberately pray that God will bring the right people into our lives, trust that vulnerability won't result in further hurt, and trust that God's love will be sufficient to heal even the deepest wounds. It's not always easy, but God calls us to trust Him with our hearts. Proverbs 3:5 encourages us to "Trust in the Lord with all your heart and lean not on your own understanding." Be deliberate in recognizing seasons when God is asking you to step out in faith and do the work it takes to build new relationships. Don't be afraid; God's got your back this time!

Practical Healing Directions: Experiencing God's Love

1. **Find a Quiet Place:** Begin by locating a quiet space where you feel safe and can truly focus. This could be a corner of your home, a peaceful garden, or anywhere you feel calm and centered. Sit comfortably, close your eyes, and take a moment to breathe deeply. With each exhale, allow any tension or anxiety to melt away, welcoming a sense of peace.

2. **Call on God:** In this sacred moment, address God in a way that feels most intimate to you such as Father, Savior, Comforter, or Friend. Speak to Him openly. Invite the Holy Spirit to fill the room, asking Him to

begin healing the wounds within you. Allow yourself to be vulnerable, opening your heart to the areas of your life where you need His love the most. Psalms 147:3 reassures us: "He heals the brokenhearted and binds up their wounds." Remember, God longs to mend your heart.

3. **Repent from revelation:** In my journey of deliverance from a spirit spouse, God revealed a deeper dimension of repentance, one rooted not just in guilt or personal failure, but in the grief my sin and my ancestors' sins caused His heart. As I repented for my own sins and the sins of my ancestors, like their idolatry, sexual sin, manipulation, and witchcraft, not because I wanted deliverance, but because I was grieved at how we had hurt God's heart, something shifted. I wasn't just seeking freedom; I was seeking to repair a relationship with my heavenly Father. And in that moment, a weight lifted. For the first time, the distance I had once felt from God was replaced with an overwhelming closeness.

As I pressed into this, the nature of my dreams shifted. Instead of sexual torment, I began having vivid dreams about my family's past through dream scenes and events I had never lived through but were later confirmed by relatives. These dreams highlighted ancestral sins that had opened spiritual doors. In obedience, I entered a season of what I call "repentance work." While salvation is by grace, this was a time of intentional partnering with the Holy Spirit to renounce inherited sins, seek God's heart, and spiritually close doors. In some cases, God led me to reach out to individuals hurt by my family's past, apologizing on behalf of my bloodline and even offering financial restitution as God led me. Those whom I called wept in healing and blessed my life. It was after one such instance that I conceived my first child. The person specifically blessed me, saying, "Because you have done this, you will carry your children." This was not to earn forgiveness but to walk in obedience and bring healing and closure to unresolved generational wounds. It became clear that repentance wasn't just for me; it was about restoring righteousness in my lineage and healing God's heart.

Imagine someone named Jimmy who is going through a similar season in his deliverance journey from a spirit spouse. He dreams that his father had once promised to marry a woman but instead married Jimmy's mom. In the dream, the woman's child she had with his dad dies, and she has another child with Jimmy's dad; a son who survives and becomes Jimmy's step-brother. In the dream, Jimmy witnesses the woman cursing the children of the woman whom his dad left her for (Jimmy's mom). Jimmy wakes up confused. After seeking counsel, he contacts an aunt who confirms that something like that happened in the past. God isn't simply asking Jimmy to apologize on behalf of his father; He's revealing a spiritual trap. By repenting for his father's actions and remaining alert, Jimmy becomes aware of patterns that could easily repeat in his own life. Jimmy is also able to break any curses upon his life that may be manifesting because of the hurt woman's curses. This is not just about healing the past but about preventing a setup to fail in the future. God was lovingly intervening to break cycles and protect Jimmy from falling into the same spirit spouse sin patterns.

Consider the following Scripture: "If my people, who are called by my name, will humble themselves and pray and seek my face and turn from their wicked ways, then I will hear from heaven, and I will forgive their sin and will heal their land" (2 Chronicles 7:14).

God desires not just to deliver us but to heal us completely. Healing comes when we are honest with God, when we allow ourselves to feel sorrow for how we have strayed, and when we embrace the joy that comes from being fully restored to Him.

As I understood this, I began to make it a personal practice to never enter God's presence without first seeking His forgiveness from a place of love and reverence. Even when invited to lead worship, I always start with songs of repentance, making space for God's mercy to flow freely as we acknowledge our need for His grace. This practice has transformed my relationship with Him and has become a powerful tool in the fight against spiritual oppression. Here are some key areas to repent of:

a. For Ancestral Sins Surrounding Love: Take a moment to acknowledge the patterns and sins that may have been passed down through generations. Repent on behalf of your ancestors for any spiritual doors they may have opened through perverted love or by withholding love. For example, if you notice that in your family line, there have been narcissistic tendencies, such as mothers not being able to love their children and thus being jealous of their children and pitting them against each other, repent, for this is a sin. In doing so, declare with conviction that these generational patterns end with you. Isaiah 61:1 says, "He has sent me to bind up the brokenhearted, to proclaim freedom for the captives."

b. For Doubt and Unbelief: Before you can fully receive God's love, you must confront any doubt or unbelief that lingers in your heart. Take a moment to repent for entertaining these thoughts. Tell God that, by faith, you choose to believe His Word. Ask the Holy Spirit to help you trust in His love completely, knowing that Jeremiah 29:11 holds true: "For I know the plans I have for you, declares the Lord, plans to prosper you and not to harm you, plans to give you hope and a future."

4. **Forgive Those Who Have Hurt You:** Reflect on the people who have caused you pain, whether knowingly or unknowingly. This may include family members, friends, or even yourself. Ask the Holy Spirit to help you forgive them from your heart, releasing the bitterness that has weighed you down. Remember, forgiveness is not about condoning their actions but about freeing yourself from their hold, as Jesus taught in Matthew 6:14-15, "For if you forgive other people

when they sin against you, your heavenly Father will also forgive you."

5. **Search the Scriptures:** Delve into the Bible for verses that speak of God's unwavering love. Choose one that resonates deeply with your heart. This Scripture will become your anchor, a truth to hold onto when doubt threatens to creep in. For instance, meditate on Romans 5:8: "But God demonstrates his own love for us in this: While we were still sinners, Christ died for us." This verse reminds us that God's love is not conditional; it is boundless.

6. **Confess the Scripture:** Make it a practice to confess this Scripture aloud three times a day. Consider it a spiritual prescription for your soul. Romans 10:17 states, "Consequently, faith comes from hearing the message, and the message is heard through the word about Christ." The more you speak God's truth over your life, the more it will penetrate your heart, transforming doubt into faith.

7. **Be Patient:** Be patient with this process, knowing that healing takes time. Philippians 1:6 reassures us, "Being confident of this, that he who began a good work in you will carry it on to completion until the day of Christ Jesus."

CONCEPT 2: LOVING GOD BACK

Understanding the need to receive God's love is only the beginning; we are called to respond. The second concept within the Key of Love is loving God back. This reciprocal relationship is vital for our spiritual growth and healing. Deuteronomy 6:5 exhorts us, "Love the Lord your God with all your heart and with all your soul and with all your strength." This is an invitation to deepen our relationship with Him, to cultivate an intimacy that allows us to experience His presence fully. When we commit to **loving God back**, we open ourselves to a transformative relationship that reshapes our identities.

Cultivating Intimacy with God

In this journey of loving God back, engaging with Him intimately becomes essential.

Psalms 145:18 declares, "The Lord is near to all who call on him, to all who call on him in truth." As we seek God earnestly, we discover the richness of His love enveloping us. James 4:8 invites us, "Come near to God and he will come near to you." This promise is profound; it indicates that our initiative in pursuing God's love is met with His readiness to embrace us. As we take steps toward Him, we create space in our hearts for His love to flourish, driving out fear, doubt, and the remnants of our past traumas. Loving God back involves learning to recognize the sound of His voice. He does not only speak in dreams or dramatic moments. He's the One who lives inside of you, always present, always speaking. Yes, He may give instructions through visions or dreams occasionally, but the voice He wants you to know most is the quiet one that whispers in your spirit every day. His voice becomes clearer as you spend time with Him by reading His Word to understand how He speaks and resting in the secret place to simply be with Him. Just like any close relationship, intimacy grows through time, attention, and love. When you begin to love God with your time and focus, you'll start to recognize Him more easily. That's how we love Him back; not just by saying it, but by choosing to be with Him.

Being Part of a Local Church Community: Being the Bride of Christ

Loving God back is more than just saying, "I love You, Lord." It's about showing that love through action, commitment, and service. One of the most powerful ways to do this is by being an active part of your local church, using your God-given gifts and talents to serve others. The church is more than just a building; it is the bride of Christ. Ephesians 5:31-32 beautifully captures this truth: "For this reason a man will leave his father and mother and be united to his wife, and the two will become one flesh. This is a profound mystery; but I am talking about Christ and the church."

The Church is a living body where each member plays a vital role. When you choose to engage, whether by teaching, singing, leading, helping the needy, or simply being there to encourage others, you are doing more than just filling a role. You are being found within "The Bride of Christ" in God's work, strengthening the faith of those around you, and reflecting His love in a tangible way. Think about it, Jesus Himself was the ultimate servant. He washed feet, fed the hungry, healed the sick, and gave His life for us. When we serve in our local church, we walk in His footsteps, showing that our faith is not just words but a lifestyle of love and sacrifice. It's in these moments of service, when you comfort someone who's hurting, when you teach a child about Jesus, when you lead worship with passion, or when you give your time to care for others, that you truly demonstrate your love for God.

The beauty of serving in church is that it not only blesses others, but it also transforms you. It deepens your relationship with God, connects you with other believers, and brings a joy that only comes from living out your purpose. You don't have to be perfect, and you don't need a grand stage. God can use whatever is in your hands, however small it may seem. The key is to step forward, to be available, and to serve with a willing heart.

So don't just sit on the sidelines. Find a place in your church where you can give, grow, and glorify God with the gifts He has placed within you. When you pour into His house, He pours into your life, and through your service, you will experience the joy of truly loving God back.

My Testimony

One day, as I was praying to God, he gave me the revelation of the fact that the spirit spouse was attacking my life because when the spirit realm looked at me, I was not found in the bride of Christ. You see, I had gone through a series of intense church hurt over and over again. I literally would get dizzy spells and panic attacks when I tried to attend a church service. God revealed to me that the church hurt had been planted in my life by the spirit spouse, and He told me I had to do two things to overcome this. Doing these two things would position me within His bride.

The first was to stop choosing a church myself and to ask Him to show me what church body He wanted me to be a part of. You see, God knows that He made us all uniquely different, and based on our background, belief systems, traumas, etc., we can only thrive in a particular church that fits our unique needs. He also knows the areas within us that He wants to heal and grow, and what church fits our current season. I believe that this is the reason why there are several different churches. God wants us all to have no excuse when it comes to being planted within one of His churches. The issues we face are because we try to pick churches that appeal to our flesh. We do not take the time to ask our all-seeing and knowing God, El Roi, to guide us to the church He chooses.

The second thing He asked me to do was to push through the spirit spouse programmed rejection at churches by confessing Scriptures against the spirit of rejection and believe Him that things would be different where He showed me to go. The two main Scriptures that gave me victory and allowed me to be planted and serve in my local church were:

Psalms 5:12, "Surely, Lord, you bless the righteous; you surround them with your favor as with a shield." And Luke 1:74-75, "To rescue us from the hand of our enemies, and to enable us to serve him without fear in holiness and righteousness before him all our days."

The church God led me to was nothing like what I would have chosen for myself, but it was everything I needed. I stepped out in faith, consistently attending church every week. At first, the closed-door syndrome of the spirit spouse tried to stop me from being accepted into a ministry, but this time, I knew who I was in Christ. I did not get hurt, feel rejected, or fall into the trap of offense. Instead, I utilized my key of warfare; I applied the prayer of agreement strategy in Mathew 19:18. I called my prayer partner, and we began to command my gates to open (Isaiah 60) to serve God at the church He had placed me in. It was not long before I got a call back from my ministry leader, and I was accepted and serving with my gifts and talents like never before. Serving God through serving people with our gifts and talents is one of the most powerful ways to defeat the spirit spouse.

By leaning on God instead of myself for wisdom on how to navigate relationships and conflicts, wielding the sword of the spirit through my daily scriptural confessions, victory became mine! Being planted within my local church as an act of love unto God brought me tremendous breakthroughs in my long but victorious battle with the spirit spouse.

CONCEPT 3: LOVING YOURSELF

As we continue our journey of love, we must pause to embrace the third concept within the key of love: loving ourselves. Many overlook this truth, focusing only on the command to love others, but the teaching of Christ in Matthew 22:39 is clear, "Love your neighbor as yourself." The key phrase here, "as yourself," reveals that self-love is not optional but essential. How can we pour love into others when our own well is dry? Without a healthy love for ourselves, any attempt to love others becomes shallow, strained, or even inauthentic.

Self-love is not selfish; it is necessary for our spiritual, emotional, and relational health. The world often confuses self-love with vanity or self-indulgence, but true self-love is rooted in recognizing our worth as children of God. Psalms 139:14 declares, "I praise you because I am fearfully and wonderfully made; your works are wonderful, I know that full well." When we internalize this truth, we begin to reject the counterfeit affections of toxic love and instead cultivate authentic relationships based on mutual respect, love, and trust.

Many individuals in this generation are ensnared by the enemy's tactics, leading them to loathe their own reflections, be it their skin, their voice, their height, or other unique attributes. This self-hate is a strategic attack designed to keep us searching for validation and love in all the wrong places, keeping us in cycles of idolatry; thus, we continue to give the spirit spouse access to oppress us. We often find ourselves seeking approval from others, convinced that their acceptance will fill the void we feel within.

My Testimony

I was born into a family where I was often told I was short, very dark-skinned, and had a big nose. These words didn't just come from strangers; they came from family members and authority figures, people whose voices I trusted. Over time, those words sank deep and shaped how I saw myself. I didn't just feel unloved; I felt unworthy. When God began to pull me out of the bondage of the spirit spouse, He didn't just deliver my soul; He began to restore my identity. He showed me that loving myself was not pride but obedience. It was aligned with His truth. He taught me to see beauty in the way He made me. I began to value my petite frame. Instead of wishing I looked like someone else, I started researching how to dress for my body type. I looked up hairstyles that suited my face shape and makeup that complemented deep, rich skin like mine. This wasn't vanity; it was healing. It was me finally saying yes to how God designed me.

As I embraced the way God made me, others began to see it, too, and verbalize it. The voices that compliment me now are far more than the voices that point out what some would consider physical flaws. I didn't change my skin, my height, or my nose; I changed my agreement. I stopped agreeing with lies and started agreeing with Heaven. That shift brought confidence and healing and new people who see me the way God sees me. If this resonates with you, here are some practical steps that helped me:

1. Discover your body shape (pear, apple, and rectangle, hourglass) and learn how to dress in a way that honors and compliments it.
2. Explore hairstyles that work with your hair texture and face shape.
3. Learn makeup techniques for your skin tone. There are many tutorials

You are fearfully and wonderfully made, and when you begin to believe that, it shows.

More Ways to Cultivate Self-Love

To cultivate self-love, we can adopt practices that nurture our relationship with ourselves. Loving oneself is a process, especially in a world filled with comparison, insecurity, and negative messages. Here are some ways to cultivate healthy, biblical self-love:

1. Acknowledge Your Worth in Christ

Our value does not come from our achievements, our possessions, or our relationships; it comes from our identity in Christ. 1 Peter 2:9 reminds us, "You are a chosen people, a royal priesthood, a holy nation, God's special possession." When we begin to see ourselves as God sees us, our perspective changes. We no longer seek validation from the world but from our Creator. This awareness frees us from seeking affection in all the wrong places, including unhealthy relationships, which lead us into negative soul ties.

2. Speak Life Over Yourself

Our words have the power to build or destroy. Proverbs 18:21 teaches, "The tongue has the power of life and death." Too often, we are our own harshest critics, speaking words of doubt, failure, and insecurity over our lives. To love ourselves means to speak life over ourselves. When you align your words with God's truth, you begin to see yourself through His eyes.

3. Celebrate Your Uniqueness

One of the greatest acts of self-love is to embrace the person God has made you to be. Psalms 139:13 says, "For You created my inmost being; you knit me together in my mother's

189

womb." This is a profound reminder that our uniqueness is intentional. We do not need to look like, act like, or be like anyone else. To love ourselves is to appreciate the distinct gifts, quirks, and qualities that make us who we are. Take some time out to discover who you are; make a list of the things that truly bring you joy and those that have the potential to irritate you. Learn who you are and understand that God seeks to express Himself uniquely through the essence of your presence.

Practice Self-Care

See self-care as a form of worship. It is a way to thank God for His workmanship. There is no one-size-fits-all self-care routine. True self-care is about tuning in to what your body, mind, and soul need and responding with love. It's about the little choices you make daily that add up to a bold, fulfilled life. Let us explore some practical ways you can engage in self-care.

Care for Your Body

- ❖ Sleep instead of scrolling. Your body repairs itself at rest. You don't need to earn it; just take it.
- ❖ Drink water instead of reaching for that third cup of coffee. Hydration fuels your body in ways caffeine never will.

- ❖ Move your body not to look a certain way, but to feel alive. Run, dance, stretch, lift, walk. Let movement be joy, not punishment.
- ❖ Eat food that makes you strong. Nourish yourself with real meals, fresh fruits, wholesome grains, and warm, comforting dishes.

Care for Your Mind

- ❖ Feed it with knowledge and inspiration. Read books, listen to music, and learn something new.
- ❖ Set boundaries. Say "No" when you need to.
- ❖ Rest your thoughts. You don't have to solve every problem in one night. You don't have to carry the weight of the world alone.
- ❖ Surround yourself with people who uplift you. Talk to a friend who gets you. Laugh. Share. Let yourself be heard.

Care for your heart

- ❖ Let yourself feel. If you're sad, cry. If you're happy, laugh out loud. If you're overwhelmed, sit in silence. Your emotions are valid. Don't bottle them up; honor them.

❖ Forgive yourself for past mistakes. Growth is messy. You are evolving. Give yourself the same grace you offer others.

❖ Let go of relationships that hurt you. If it drains you, if it belittles you, if it makes you question your worth, it's not love.

Care for Your Spirit

❖ Step outside. Stand barefoot on the earth. Feel the wind, watch the sky. Let nature remind you that life is bigger than your worries.

❖ Ask yourself the big questions: What do I truly want? What makes me come alive? God has placed the answers already within you, so listen.

❖ Identify what sets your soul on fire and make time to engage in it. Sing, paint, travel, write, and create. Life is not meant to be lived on autopilot.

CONCEPT 4: LOVING OTHERS

The fourth concept within the key of love is loving others. One of the most powerful manifestations of God's love is the ability to extend it to others. Romans 5:5 tells us, "God's love has been poured out into our hearts through the Holy Spirit, who has been given to us." This love, divine in origin, is not meant to remain within us. It is meant to overflow, touching the lives of others around us. We are vessels, called to share the love we have received from God, and in doing so, we create a ripple effect that breaks the chains of isolation and darkness that spirit spouses and other demonic forces thrive upon.

1 John 4:19 reminds us, "We love because He first loved us." The love we extend to others is a direct response to the love we have already received. This flow of love creates an environment where healing, deliverance, and restoration can flourish. It dismantles the strongholds that the enemy builds through division, fear, and rejection.

When Jesus commanded us to love our neighbors as ourselves, He was inviting us into a deeper reflection of God's heart. John 13:34-35 says, "A new command I give you: Love one another. As I have loved you, you must love one another. By this everyone will know that you are my disciples, if you love one another." The love we show to others becomes a living testimony of the love we have received from God, and this kind of love is a powerful spiritual weapon.

Some Practical Ways to Love Others

1. **Ask God to give you His eyes for people:** Real love begins in the spirit. Pray that God will give you His heart for others so you can see their pain, their value, and their story. Sometimes, the most difficult people

are the ones who are hurting the most. When we ask God to bring their backstory to life in our hearts, we become less judgmental and tenderer.

2. **Speak with kindness and restraint:** True love thinks before it speaks. Avoid making fun of others' physical features or using sarcasm as a social tool. Ask yourself, is what I'm saying edifying? Would I want someone to say this about me or my child? As Ephesians 4:29 reminds us, "Do not let any unwholesome talk come out of your mouths, but only what is helpful for building others up according to their needs." Words carry weight. Choose to use yours to heal, not harm.

3. **Minister from your healed places:** If you've healed from the pain of having experienced lack in an area like growing up without nurturing love from a parent, ask God to show you others who are experiencing that same lack. You are uniquely equipped to pour into them what you once longed for. If you lacked a mother's care, become that loving figure to someone younger. If you have overcome something like difficulty getting married or even childbirth, seek out someone to partner with in prayer and encouragement

who is on a similar journey to the one you have successfully navigated. Healing multiplies when we give away what God has restored in us.

4. **Love others in their own language:** Discover the love languages of those around you, whether it's words of affirmation, quality time, acts of service, gifts, or physical touch. Don't just love people how you like to be loved; love them how they need to be loved. This takes humility and attentiveness, but it makes your love real and felt.

5. **Care for the vulnerable:** Be intentional about blessing orphans, widows, and those often forgotten. This can be through donations, volunteering, mentorship, or simple acts of care. James 1:27 calls this "pure religion." God's love shines brightly when we reach down and lift those in need.

6. **Be a friend:** Friendship is a ministry of presence. Sometimes, just showing up, calling someone to check in, or offering a small, thoughtful gift can break down walls. Giving is a practical and powerful expression of love. It doesn't have to be expensive, just intentional.

THE KEY OF JOY

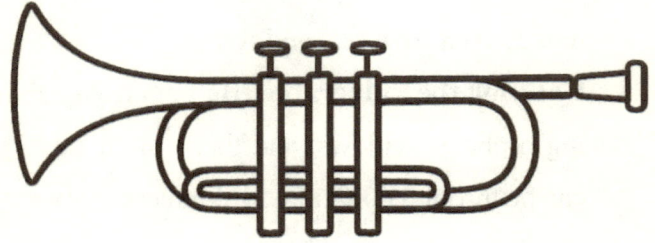

Color in: Yellow

CHAPTER 6

THE KEY OF JOY

Joy is far more than an emotion; it is a weapon forged in the very heart of God. In the midst of spiritual warfare, joy becomes a source of supernatural strength that confounds the enemy. The Bible declares, "The joy of the Lord is your strength" (Nehemiah 8:10). This joy is not a fleeting feeling based on external circumstances but is a deep, abiding confidence in God's sovereignty and love. When we embrace God's supernatural joy, it becomes a fortified stronghold within our hearts to defeat the spirit spouse.

When we stand in joy, especially during adversity, we make a bold declaration that we trust God's promises over the enemy's lies. Joy becomes an act of defiance against the darkness that seeks to overwhelm us. It says, "I may be facing trials, but I choose to rejoice in my God, who is greater than any circumstance." This choice to embrace joy is not an act of ignorance but a powerful affirmation of our faith. It allows us to rise above our present challenges and see them through the lens of God's eternal perspective.

The supernatural nature of joy also extends to those around us. When we choose joy, in spite of our circumstances, we become conduits of God's light, shining brightly in a world often shrouded in darkness. Our joy can inspire others, offering them hope in their struggles. Every human being will face trials. What really sets us apart as Christians is exhibiting "The Joy of the Lord." As we choose to manifest joy in our character and habits, we encourage those who may be wrestling with despair but who do not know Christ to seek to develop a relationship with Him.

How to Choose Joy

1. Accept That There Will Be Hard Times

James 1:2-3 encourages us: "Consider it pure joy, my brothers and sisters, whenever you face trials of many kinds, because you know that the testing of your faith produces perseverance." This Scripture says "whenever"; it does not say "if." It is a guarantee that we will face trials. Finding joy in times of difficulty is not a natural response; it is a deliberate choice. Joy is not a denial of hardship but a recognition that God is at work, even in the most trying of circumstances. It is a declaration that our hope rests not in our situation, but in the One who controls it.

During my own deliverance journey, joy was a lifeline. There were days when the spiritual attacks felt relentless, when the lies of the enemy seemed louder than God's truth. Yet, I made the choice to praise God, to sing in the face of oppression. I had the courage to do this because I found the grace through Christ to accept that living out our human experience involves "hard times." The more I chose joy, the more I felt God's peace flood my spirit, even when my circumstances had not yet changed.

2. Embrace Contentment

Contentment is a spiritual posture that fortifies the soul with joy and peace, making it difficult for demonic influences such as spirit spouses to find a foothold. The Bible says in 1 Timothy 6:6, "But godliness with contentment is great gain," reminding us that spiritual wealth is found not in striving, but in resting in God's provision. Spirit spouses often exploit dissatisfaction, loneliness, or unresolved desires, using them as open doors. But when a believer embraces true contentment in Christ, those doors begin to close. Philippians 4:11-13 offers Paul's powerful testimony, "I have learned the secret of being content in any and every situation… I can do all this through him who gives me strength." Cultivating contentment daily can include practical habits like giving thanks out loud for both small and large blessings, avoiding comparison by limiting time on social media, meditating on Scriptures that affirm your identity in Christ, and intentionally celebrating spiritual growth rather than focusing on unmet desires. When joy and contentment take root, the soul becomes grounded in God's presence, and that kind of joy is a weapon that confuses and repels the enemy.

This prayer will help you.

Heavenly Father, I come before you in humility and repentance. I acknowledge that I have entertained the spirit of discontent by allowing comparison, complaint, and ungratefulness to take root in my heart. I repent for every thought, word, and attitude that dishonored your provision and timing. I renounce every agreement I made, knowingly or unknowingly, with the spirit of discontent, and I break its influence over my life in Jesus' name.

In the name of Jesus, I now declare that I am satisfied in Christ alone. I receive the joy of the Lord as my strength and the peace of God as my guard. I choose gratitude over grumbling, faith over frustration, and worship over worry. My heart is anchored in the truth that God is enough for me. I close every door that was opened through restlessness or longing outside of His will. I am whole, I am loved, and I am free. Amen.

3. Confess Scripture out loud instead of complaining

Confess this powerful Scripture as many times a day as you need to until you feel the heaviness lifting. "The joy of the Lord is my strength" (Nehemiah 8:10). This powerful Scripture is a cornerstone of faith, but it goes deeper than just a comforting phrase. It is a portal for us to experience a joy that gives us strength. A joy that is not reliant on circumstances, emotions, or even our own resilience. Joy, in its essence, is not happiness. While happiness fluctuates with the ups and downs of life, joy remains steadfast, rooted in the unchanging nature of God. The only way to truly experience this is to use the Word of God as a straw to pull joy from God into you.

This understanding of joy is one of the keys that helped me overcome severe anxiety and strange phobias, all of which the spirit spouse had erected in my life. I recall one day, after yet another attack, crying out to God in frustration. I had gone through deliverance but still found myself facing this enemy. It was at that moment that God gave me my second single called **Joy Song**, with the very words from Nehemiah 8:10, which I sang daily, and this brought me freedom.

4. Practice deliberate and mindful thanksgiving

As we express gratitude for God's blessings, we position our hearts to receive His joy more fully. We must discipline our minds to see our cups as half full always. No matter how bad we might think our situation is, there is always something we can be thankful for. I remember when God was instilling this practice in me; I would thank Him out loud throughout the day for the seemingly mundane things we take for granted each day like, breathing, talking, hearing, and having a roof over our heads. If your brain has been so battered by a spirit of despair, I encourage you to start cultivating the practice of writing down what you are grateful for each day and reading out what you have written to God. As you do this, you will notice the supernatural joy of God fill your heart.

Stay in community

Joy flourishes in the context of community and fellowship. When we gather with others, whether in worship, prayer, or simple companionship, we amplify our individual experiences of joy. Acts of service and kindness can also be avenues through which joy flows, as we reflect God's love to others. Stepping out of ourselves to minister unto someone who needs us allows us to shift our focus from our own problems. The very act of being a blessing to another will open us up to experience God's supernatural joy. Collective worship, where voices unite in praise, cultivates an atmosphere rich in joy, reinforcing our connection with God and each other. Pause here and say a prayer asking God to connect you with "**Your Kind**," people with whom you share the same values and enjoy similar things. He is faithful, and He will connect you with them.

5. Indulge your inner child

The playful side of you is your inner child. Sit with God and ask Him to remind you of the things that brought you joy as a child and which bring laughter to your soul. Make a deliberate effort to do them. Sometimes, after years of oppression, we forget who we are and what makes us thrive. Be deliberate in engaging in activities that bring you a sense of fulfillment and purpose. Joy can be harnessed through creativity, whether through art, music, dance, or other forms of expression, like caring for animals, starting a garden, joining a choir, learning to play an instrument you wished you had learned to play as a child, playing a board game with a loving family member or friend, going to a night of clean comedy to belly laugh, etc.

6. Regulate your nervous system

Years of trauma and demonic oppression can leave one with symptoms of a dysregulated nervous system, such as panic attacks, insomnia, depression, gut issues, chronic body pain, dizziness, and feeling constantly on edge. Practices like taking just five minutes three times a day to engage in deep breathing, taking walks in nature, getting sunlight, and drinking relaxing teas like chamomile or lemon balm tea can help us to heal and experience joy.

7. Celebrate intentionally with food and fellowship

In Nehemiah 8:10, the people were told to eat choice food and sweet drinks. "Nehemiah said, "Go and enjoy choice food and sweet drinks, and send some to those who have nothing prepared. This day is holy to our Lord. Do not grieve, for the joy of the Lord is your strength." Joy can be experienced through intentional celebration. Celebrate birthdays and special occasions. Families that have been tormented by spirit spouses usually find it hard to celebrate. This was something God had to break over my life, and as I leaned on Him, I overcame the spirit that tried to make me either ignore special days or get sick if I decided to celebrate them. Remember, celebrating does not always have to be a big feast. Cooking or sharing a favorite meal with loved ones or even preparing something special just for you will invite a supernatural atmosphere of joy. It's not about indulgence but about marking spiritual victories, seasons of breakthroughs, or simply enjoying God's goodness. Don't forget to share with others who may not have because joy multiplies when it's shared.

8. Draw strength from the wells of salvation and the hope of eternal life

Isaiah 12:3 beautifully illustrates this truth: "With joy you will draw water from the wells of salvation." This Scripture reminds us that choosing a posture of joy allows us to access the life-giving waters of God's ultimate salvation from eternal damnation through Christ, refreshing our souls even in the heat of battle.

To do this, shift your focus from the temporal to the eternal, recognizing that our identity is rooted not in our present challenges but in the finished work of Christ on the cross. Bring to your memory and meditate on Scripture that assures you that no matter what happens in this present life, you have been granted eternal life through Christ Jesus. Consider 2 Corinthians 4:17, which states, "For our light and momentary troubles are achieving for us an eternal glory that far outweighs them all." Shifting your thinking to eternity has the power of flooding your soul with supernatural endurance for the present circumstance you may be facing and keeping you operating in joy instead of doom and despair.

THE KEY OF
WORSHIP

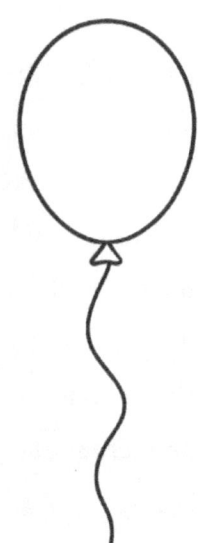

Color in: Blue

CHAPTER 7

THE KEY OF WORSHIP

My Testimony

In my own journey, I have felt the life-altering power of worship during my darkest days. When the weight of anxiety and fear pressed down like heavy fog, and the spirit spouse visits came daily in spite of prayer, I turned to worship as my lifeline. In those moments when despair threatened to engulf me, I began to pour out my heart in songs of adoration. With every note sung, I felt the oppressive darkness begin to lift. It was as if my worship ignited a spiritual fire, driving back the shadows that had taken residence in my soul. I found strength and hope as God's presence enveloped me, reminding me that He was ever so close, ready to fight for my freedom.

Consider the story of Paul and Silas, two men who found themselves imprisoned for their faith. In Acts 16:25-26, we witness a powerful moment of worship and joy in the darkest of circumstances. Despite being chained and facing uncertain futures, Paul and Silas chose to lift their voices in praise to God. Their decision to worship was not just a reaction to their plight; it was a deliberate choice rooted in their unwavering trust in God's goodness.

As they sang hymns, worship permeated the prison walls, and a miraculous earthquake ensued. The foundations of the prison shook, chains fell off, and doors swung open. In that moment, worship became their liberating force, turning their captivity into freedom. The enemy had thought he could silence them, but their joyful worship not only brought personal deliverance but also served as a testament to the power of God at work.

Worship creates an atmosphere conducive to healing. One of the symptoms of the spirit spouse is "strange infirmity." In my case, this was rooted in "Inherited Health Anxiety," which is a belief in a lie that we need to control our health. Health anxiety torments the individual with obsessive thoughts, which are based on lies about getting sick or dying prematurely from sickness. What helps is to refocus our minds on God and His sovereignty over every aspect of our lives, including our health. Worship provides a platform for us to confront the very lies that a spirit spouse would use to manipulate and oppress us. When we sing praises, recite Scripture, and lift our voices in adoration, we surround ourselves with the truth of God's Word. In Isaiah 61:3, we are reminded that God gives us "a crown of beauty instead of ashes, the oil of joy instead of mourning, and a garment of praise instead of a spirit of despair." Worship transforms our mourning into joy, and it is in that transformation that we find the strength to break free from the clutches of a spirit spouse.

Additionally, worship drives out the spirit of fear, which is one of the biggest weapons the spirit spouse uses as an open door to entangle its victims, but we can cultivate an intimate relationship with God through worship, allowing us to receive His love and affirmation. In Romans 8:15, we are reminded that we have not received a spirit of fear, but of adoption, enabling us to cry out, "Abba, Father!" As we worship, we embrace this identity, reclaiming our place as beloved children of God. This understanding empowers us to break free from the grip of a spirit spouse, which seeks to rob us of our worth and identity.

Types Of Worship

The Secret Place: Personal Worship A Powerful Weapon Against the Spirit Spouse. We read about this place in Psalm 91. This isn't just a quiet corner for prayer; it's a lifeline for every believer. It is where divine encounters happen, where chains are broken, and where those who truly seek God are filled with His power. The secret place is not about religion or routine. It is about intimacy. It is where you don't just talk to God; you become one with Him.

Many desire miracles, breakthroughs, and answered prayers, but few understand that everything in the Kingdom is birthed in the secret place. Every victory you see in the physical was first won in the spiritual. This is why Jesus Himself made time to be alone with the Father. Mark 1:35 tells us, "Very early in the morning, while it was still dark, Jesus got up, left the house and went off to a solitary place, where He prayed." He understood something many Christians today do not; if you want to walk in power and victory, you must dwell in the secret place. But here's what many don't realize, the secret place is not just a place of divine encounters. It is also one of the greatest battlegrounds. There is a war over your intimacy because whoever owns your secret place owns your life and destiny.

Just as God desires deep intimacy with His children in the secret place of their hearts, the enemy has created a counterfeit, a dark, deceptive force that we've been talking about known as the spirit spouse. This demonic entity mimics divine intimacy, union, and communion, seeking to steal what belongs to God through sexual dream encounters. The spirit spouse infiltrates dreams, stirs unholy desires, and binds people in cycles of delay, disappointment, and spiritual dryness. It is a demonic claim over the secret places of a person's soul, seeking to corrupt their relationship and oneness with God in order to distort their destiny.

The enemy understands something most believers ignore. True power comes from intimacy. If he can corrupt your secret place, he can control your life. If you are intimate with God, you walk in victory, breakthrough, and divine favor because you are not alone but one with God. But if you unknowingly engage demonic generational covenants through sexual dreams, which lead to entertaining unholy desires in the secret places of your soul, you give the enemy legal ground to operate in your life because they are your legal spouse in the secret place. They are the ones receiving your love, affection, and time! So you must resist the devil and not tolerate this perversion he is trying to establish within you.

The question is not whether you are intimate with something in the spirit, but the question is, Who are you intimate with?

This is why Jesus tells us in Matthew 6:6, "When you pray, go into your room, close the door, and pray to your Father, who is unseen. Then your Father, who sees what is done in secret, will reward you." Your rewards of breakthrough, healing, and victory are hidden in the secret place. **Who owns your secret place?** What happens in your life when it is quiet, and you think no one is watching? Have you let depression in and not resisted? Have you let the love of money in? Have you let masturbation in? Have you let anxiety in? Have you let people-pleasing in? Have you let overeating in? Have you let homosexuality in? Have you let narcissism in? Have you let the love of fame in? Have you let pornography in? There is power to resist in Christ. Get up! It is not too late. Resist and hand over your secret place to God by cultivating your secret place with the help of the Holy Spirit.

Cultivating Your Secret Place: A Life of Divine Intimacy.

1. Make Time for God Daily

God desires consistency, not convenience. Set aside a specific time daily to meet with Him. It could be early in the morning, during breaks, or at night. What matters is that you show up.

2. Repent and Keep Your Heart Pure

Sin creates distance between you and God. Repentance cleanses your heart and restores intimacy. Ask the Holy Spirit to reveal anything that hinders your relationship with Him daily.

"If we confess our sins, He is faithful and just to forgive us and to cleanse us from all unrighteousness" (1 John 1:9).

3. Create a Sacred Atmosphere

Find a quiet place where you can focus on God. It could be your room, a prayer closet, or even a quiet walk. Turn off distractions, play worship music, and let your heart be still before Him.

"Be still and know that I am God" (Psalm 46:10).

4. Feed on the Word of God

Your secret place is built on the Word. Read the Bible daily, meditate on Scripture, and let it renew your mind. God speaks through His Word, giving wisdom, strength, and direction.

"Your word is a lamp to my feet and a light to my path" (Psalm 119:105).

5. Practice Silence and Listening

Many people talk to God but never pause to listen. Listening is actually the essence of the secret place. After praying, take time to be silent. God often speaks in "a still, small voice" (1 Kings 19:12). He may drop a thought, a Scripture, or a deep peace in your spirit. If your time with God is 30 mins, I recommend you do not give God less than 15 mins of listening time. Even if you are still talking, listen for His promptings for you to pause and listen.

6. Guard Your Intimacy with God

Distractions, sinful habits, and worldly influences can pull you away from the secret place. Be intentional about protecting your time with God. Remove anything that competes with Him.

Congregational Worship

Congregational worship is a beautiful expression of unity and collective devotion, where believers gather as a community to lift their voices and hearts in praise and honor to God. This sacred assembly is more than just a routine; it is a powerful encounter with the Divine that amplifies our individual experiences and deepens our connection to one another.

In Hebrews 10:25, we are reminded of the importance of not neglecting to meet together, as the fellowship of believers enriches our spiritual journey. When we come together in worship, the atmosphere shifts; it transforms into a sacred space where the presence of God is palpable. The collective worship experience not only uplifts our spirits but also serves to encourage and strengthen us in our faith.

Moreover, congregational worship opens the door to powerful encounters with God. As we lift our hands and hearts in unison, we invite His presence to dwell among us. It is in these moments of collective surrender that lives are transformed, healing occurs, and chains of bondage are broken.

Lifestyle Worship

Lifestyle worship is the profound understanding that our devotion to God extends far beyond the confines of church services or specific moments of singing. It is this aspect of worship that brings a long-lasting breakthrough from the spirit spouse. It is a holistic approach to living that integrates our reverence and obedience to God into every aspect of our daily lives. Romans 12:1 beautifully encapsulates this idea, urging us to "present our bodies as living sacrifices, holy and pleasing to God." This Scripture invites us to consider our entire being, our thoughts, actions, and intentions, as instruments of worship.

Every day, we encounter countless opportunities to worship God through our choices and behaviors. Whether we are at work, in our homes, or engaging with others in our communities, the way we conduct ourselves can be a testament to our faith. This call to lifestyle worship transforms the ordinary into the extraordinary, reminding us that even the most mundane tasks can be elevated to acts of worship when done with a heart aligned with God.

For instance, when we approach our work with integrity, excellence, and a servant's heart, we honor God in our professional lives. Colossians 3:23 encourages us to "work at it with all your heart, as working for the Lord, not for human masters," reminding us that our everyday efforts are not merely about fulfilling obligations but can be an offering of worship.

Lifestyle worship calls us to engage in relationships with love and compassion. When we treat others with kindness, respect, and humility, we embody the love of Christ and exemplify the values of His Kingdom. Each interaction becomes an opportunity to showcase the light of Christ, fostering a culture of grace and understanding. Matthew 5:16 encourages us to "let your light shine before others, that they may see your good deeds and glorify your Father in heaven."

In our homes, lifestyle worship takes on a special significance. When we create an atmosphere of love, patience, and encouragement, we reflect God's nature within our families. Acts of service, expressions of gratitude, and moments of prayer can transform our households into places of worship. By intentionally incorporating spiritual practices, such as reading

Scripture, sharing testimonies, or praying together, we establish a rhythm of worship that permeates our everyday lives.

Additionally, lifestyle worship extends to our leisure activities and hobbies. Whether through the arts, sports, or community service, we can engage in pursuits that reflect our passion for God and His creation. By using our gifts and talents to serve others, we align our personal joys with a higher purpose, recognizing that every passion can be an avenue for glorifying God.

Ultimately, lifestyle worship is about surrendering our entire lives to God and recognizing that every moment is an opportunity to honor Him. It requires intentionality and a willingness to see our daily routines as sacred spaces where we can encounter His presence. When we fully embrace this call to live as a living sacrifice, we cultivate a life that continuously praises and worships God in all things, revealing the depth of our relationship with Him to the world around us.

How to Practice Worship

1. Seek Out Worship Nights and Environments of Worship

Surround yourself with others who are hungry for God's presence. Worship nights are places where the atmosphere is already set, and your spirit can connect more easily. Being in a community during worship builds faith and creates spiritual momentum. The spirit spouse hates worship nights because these are nights when the presence of God saturates the atmosphere and makes it uncomfortable. "God inhabits the praises of His people" (Psalm 22:3).

2. Be Deliberate About Worshiping with Musical Instruments and Singing

God loves it when we sing to Him accompanied by musical instruments. Psalm 100:1–2, "Shout for joy to the Lord, all the earth. Worship the Lord with gladness; come before him with joyful songs." Psalm 150:3–5, "Praise him with the sounding of the trumpet... with the harp and lyre... with timbrel and dancing... with strings and pipe... with the clash of cymbals...." But don't only wait for church service. Create your own worship moments using music and instruments, even if it's just your voice and a tambourine. I am personally committed to giving God one hour every week on Thursdays when I sing songs of praise and worship to Him in my secret place, accompanied by a tambourine or the African shekere. I believe that maintaining this practice has helped to maintain my deliverance from the spirit spouse, but most importantly, it has been a time of experiencing God's presence in a tangible way. If you've always wanted to learn a musical instrument, now is the time. Learn it and use it in your private worship time with God. You can also partner with a ministry or church that hosts regular worship nights solely dedicated to honoring God through worship. Consider supporting them financially, especially the musicians, as quality worship requires resources. Sponsoring worship gatherings is a powerful way to worship God with musical instruments, even if you're not the one playing. You're helping create an atmosphere for His presence to dwell.

3. Be Expressive in Your Worship

Use your whole body to worship. Most Christians don't know that God does not expect our worship to be just internal. He expects that it should involve our whole bodies. Bow, kneel, lift your hands and dance. These are physical postures of surrender and love that deeply move God's heart and make Him happy. Don't be afraid to be visible in your worship. Expressing love to God is never wasted or foolish. The Bible gives us specific examples of what God expects us to do with our body parts during worship.

- ❖ Lift your hands: Psalm 134:2, "Lift up your hands in the sanctuary and praise the Lord."
- ❖ Bow and Kneel: Psalm 95:6, "Come, let us bow down in worship, let us kneel before the Lord our Maker."
- ❖ Dance: 2 Samuel 6:14, "Wearing a linen ephod, David was dancing before the Lord with all his might."
- ❖ Clap your hands: Psalm 47:1, "Clap your hands, all you nations; shout to God with cries of joy."
- ❖ Shout with your voice: Psalm 100:1, "Shout for joy to the LORD, all the earth."

If you struggle with a spirit spouse and you do not already engage in worshiping God in this manner, I advise you to begin to do this. This was one of the areas in my journey that, when I began to lean into practically, brought me a great breakthrough and helped me feel the tangible presence of God. This is especially helpful for those who struggle with feeling God's love.

4. Worship in Spirit and in Truth

Worship isn't just about music. It is about the posture of your heart. Come before God with honesty, vulnerability, and complete surrender. Don't hold back your tears, especially in seasons of pain or hardship. God is drawn to the broken and contrite. He honors the worshiper who comes with tears more than the one who appears "put together" but is distant and disengaged. Invite the Holy Spirit to lead your worship. Let it flow from a deep place of truth and Spirit-filled intimacy. "The true worshipers will worship the Father in the Spirit and in truth, for they are the kind of worshipers the Father seeks" (John 4:23–24).

5. Make Worship a Daily Lifestyle

Worship isn't just for Sunday. It is every day. Speak well of God, and sing to Him in your home, in your car, and on your walks. Keep worship music playing. Let it become the soundtrack of your life. Psalm 34:1, "I will extol the Lord at all times; his praise will always be on my lips."

THE KEY OF GRACE

Color in: Red

CHAPTER 8

———— ❦ ————

THE KEY OF GRACE

My Testimony

In my own journey of deliverance from a spirit spouse, I reached a point where I felt stuck. I needed the key of grace to set me free! You see, the spirit spouse had been cast out of my life, but it still had an open door to come back whenever it wanted to torment me because I had not yet received the revelation of God's grace. I was operating with him from the mindset that I believed that I needed to work hard to earn deliverance from him. A religious spirit stronghold lied to me that I was not doing enough to be free; it convinced me that I needed to wear only skirts, tie up my hair, and pray for a particular length of time and that I just needed to do more so I could be completely free. At this stage of my journey, the spirit spouse episodes took a turn and became even more vicious than before. I began to genuinely cry out to God; I could not understand how this was happening. I was being the best Christian I thought I could be; I even looked down on other Christians who I did not see putting themselves through the rigorous religious disciplines that I endured, but the symptoms of the spirit spouse persisted to the point of a near-death experience, which was shown to me by the taunting spirit spouse before it occurred.

Despite months of fasting and prayer, I lay on a surgery table with my life slipping away due to complications resulting from the birth of my 3rd child. That was the day Jesus delivered me from a religious spirit. At that moment, I was weighed down by the memory of past failures and accusations from religious authority figures. In desperation, I cried out to God, laying bare my pain and regrets; as I did this, I felt an overwhelming sense of God's presence and his gentle reminder that His grace was enough. 2 Corinthians 12:9 echoed in my heart: "My grace is sufficient for you, for My power is made perfect in weakness." This verse was a reminder that God wasn't asking me to be perfect; He simply wanted my heart and trust. As I embraced this truth, a deep shift happened within me. Even though I was crawling through the valley of death, I felt lighter, renewed, and hopeful.

As I struggled for my life that day, it dawned on me that there was no amount of "good works" that would give me right standing before a "Just God." I received His grace when shocked doctors (in between several surgical procedures being done to save my life) informed me that I was medically barren.

They stated that, based on their findings, it was a miracle that I had conceived 3 children naturally. I held on to their words as I fought for my life by believing that the God who had miraculously given me children could heal me without my help. I had come to the end of myself. I had no strength left to do any of the religious activities I used to believe could save me. I had no other choice but to simply cling to the God of Ephesians 2:8 and truly take Him for His Word, which states that I am saved by grace. After I was discharged from the hospital, the chains of oppression and depression began to fall off as I accepted that I needed physical and emotional help; I was set free to accept God's grace in the form of therapists and counselors, something that the religious mindset had held me back from enjoying.

The Mystery of Grace

Grace is a divine mystery. It is God's unearned love, mercy, and kindness extended to us daily. It breaks demonic bondage, heals wounds, and empowers us to live in freedom. Grace is not based on our worthiness but on God's unconditional love.

Ephesians 2:8–9 reminds us, "It is by grace you have been saved... it is the gift of God." We can't earn it or understand it fully. Grace defies logic and invites us to rest in God's love, not our performance. Romans 5:8 tells us that grace sought us out before we even knew we needed it. Long before we turned to God, He turned to us, offering forgiveness, healing, and restoration. Psalm 103:12 says, "He removes our sins as far as the east is from the west." Grace doesn't excuse our sins; it transforms them and invites us into deeper intimacy with God. In this new place of intimacy, we do not want to hurt God, and He helps us to fulfill this desire by His Spirit. Lamentations 3:22–23 tells us, "His mercies are new every morning." Grace meets us daily, offering a fresh start and renewed strength, no matter yesterday's failures. Grace also calls us to extend what we've received. Colossians 3:13 commands us to "forgive as the Lord forgave you." Grace doesn't stop with us; it flows through us to others. Ultimately, grace redeems. Romans 8:28 assures us that "God works all things for good." He turns pain into purpose.

God Has Given Every Believer Great Grace

"And with great power gave the apostles witness of the resurrection of the Lord Jesus: and great grace was upon them all" (Acts 4:33).

Grace is more than a gentle gift from God; it is a powerful force that enables us to fight battles we cannot win on our own. In Philippians 4:13, Paul proclaims, "I can do all things through him who gives me strength." This verse highlights how grace infuses us with supernatural strength, equipping us to tackle challenges that would be impossible by our own means.

One of grace's powerful roles is to strengthen us when we feel weakest. 2 Corinthians 12:9 provides this reassurance, as God tells Paul, "My grace is sufficient for you, for my power is made perfect in weakness." Often, in the battle against spiritual forces, we may feel intimidated, discouraged, or overwhelmed by our own limitations. Yet, it is precisely in our moments of weakness that grace becomes most powerful. Grace steps in as our defender, filling us with a resolve that no power of darkness can shake.

Many who haven't received the revelation of grace often fall into a religious spirit focused on performance over relationship. This opens the door to the spirit spouse, allowing emotional, mental, and even physical affliction to take root. But when grace is embraced, chains break, healing flows and freedom begins.

The Religious Spirit: A Major Barrier to Experiencing God's Grace

A religious spirit is a deceptive influence that distorts true faith, replacing a personal relationship with God with rigid rules, traditions, and self-righteousness. It operates under the guise of holiness but is actually a counterfeit, leading people away from the freedom found in Christ. Unlike blatant sins such as immorality or greed, the religious spirit hides behind a mask of godliness. It whispers that obeying religious rules is more important than knowing God personally. It convinces people that they are righteous because of their outward devotion while keeping them spiritually dry on the inside. The Pharisees in Jesus' time were the perfect example of this. They memorized Scripture, observed the Law to the letter, and were considered the religious elite. Yet, Jesus called them "white-washed tombs," clean on the outside but full of death on the inside (Matthew 23:27).

How the Spirit Spouse Manifests as a Religious Spirit

While most people associate spirit spouses with relationship struggles, sexual dreams, and marital delays, these spirits also operate on a deeper and more dangerous level, through religion.

1. Opposition to True Deliverance, Resisting Spiritual Freedom

One of the strongest indicators of a religious spirit is an aversion to true deliverance. Those under its influence often feel an inexplicable resistance to deep prayer, fasting, and seeking help for their struggles. The religious spirit, working through the spirit spouse, plants deceptive thoughts like:

- ❖ "You don't need deliverance; only weak Christians seek that."
- ❖ "You're already saved; why waste time on spiritual warfare?"
- ❖ "These deliverance ministers are too dramatic; just pray quietly."

As a result, the person may believe that deliverance is unnecessary or even unbiblical. They may avoid teachings on spiritual warfare, dismiss testimonies of others who have been set free, or feel uncomfortable when topics of demonic bondage and deliverance arise. Even when they try to engage in prayer, they often experience overwhelming distractions, fatigue, or mental fog. Some feel an invisible force hindering them from praying deeply. Others fall asleep instantly when they try to read the Bible or attend church services but stay wide awake during entertainment. This resistance is a clear sign of a spirit spouse at work, ensuring that its victim remains spiritually weak and unable to break free from its grip.

2. False Holiness, the Deception of Outward Righteousness

A religious spirit does not lead to true holiness but a distorted version of it. People under its influence often focus more on external appearances than internal transformation. They may take pride in their long prayers, strict fasting schedules, or dressing modestly but struggle with deeper sins like bitterness, envy, or lust. Their faith becomes a performance rather than a genuine relationship with God. Legalism becomes their identity. They measure their spirituality by what they do rather than who they are in Christ. Some signs of this include:

- Being obsessed with religious rituals like Sabbath days and biblical festivals and traditions but lacking personal intimacy with God. Colossians 2:16–17, "Therefore do not let anyone judge you by what you eat or drink, or with regard to a religious festival, a New Moon celebration or a Sabbath day. These are a shadow of the things that were to come; the reality, however, is found in Christ."
- Judging others harshly based on external actions rather than the condition of their hearts.

Ironically, many who struggle with a spirit spouse suffer from hidden sexual temptations or emotional instability. Despite their outward righteousness, they often battle private sins that contradict the image they portray. The spirit spouse ensures that they remain bound, trapped in an exhausting cycle of striving for holiness but never achieving true spiritual freedom.

3. Guilt and Condemnation, the Unending Cycle of Shame

One of the most dangerous tactics of a spirit spouse is keeping its victims trapped in guilt and self-condemnation. Instead of experiencing the conviction of the Holy Spirit, which leads to repentance and transformation, they live under constant fear of never being good enough for God.

- ❖ They often feel like their prayers are ineffective.
- ❖ They believe they must "earn" God's love by working harder.
- ❖ They are tormented by thoughts that they have sinned too much to be forgiven.
- ❖ They live in constant fear of divine punishment.

This makes them fall into performance-based Christianity, where their relationship with God is driven by fear rather than love. The spirit spouse thrives in this environment, feeding off their insecurities. It convinces them that they will never be truly free, keeping them bound in an exhausting cycle of striving without rest.

4. Spiritual Pride, the Illusion of Superiority

Another common sign of a religious spirit is spiritual arrogance. Some people, under the influence of a spirit spouse, develop a sense of superiority over others. They measure their spirituality by how much they pray, fast, or know the Bible rather than by the fruit of the Holy Spirit in their lives.

They may look down on those who:

❖ Do not follow the same religious routines as they do.

❖ Struggle with sins they believe they have conquered.

❖ Attend churches they consider "less spiritual."

Despite this outward confidence, many secretly battle deep struggles in their personal lives. Many experience:

❖ Unexplained delays in marriage or constant relationship breakdowns.

❖ Emotional detachment in existing relationships.

❖ Sudden spiritual dryness despite religious activities.

The religious spirit blinds them from recognizing that these struggles are signs of bondage. Instead of seeking deliverance, they convince themselves that their suffering is a sign of a "higher spiritual calling." This pride keeps them from acknowledging their need for freedom.

5. Manipulation and Control, Forcing Religion on Others

The religious spirit often leads to controlling behavior. People under its influence become obsessed with making others conform to their version of Christianity.

- ❖ They dictate how others should pray, dress, and worship.
- ❖ They use fear and guilt to manipulate people into religious activities.
- ❖ They believe that unless someone follows their exact doctrine, they are not truly saved.

Instead of allowing the Holy Spirit to guide people, they take on the role of "spiritual police," enforcing rules and traditions without grace. This is exactly how the Pharisees operated during Jesus' time, burdening people with religious laws while missing the heart of God's message. At its core, this control stems from the spirit spouse's influence, ensuring that its victim remains trapped in a cycle of judgment rather than love, fear rather than faith, and religion rather than relationship.

6. Opposition to the Holy Spirit

Perhaps the most dangerous aspect of the religious spirit is that it resists the move of God. Whenever the Holy Spirit moves in power, bringing revival, miracles, and deep transformation, this spirit rises in opposition. It uses skepticism, fear, and tradition to quench the fire of God. The Pharisees saw Jesus heal the sick, raise the dead, and cast out demons, yet they called Him a blasphemer. They were so committed to their religious traditions that they missed the Messiah standing in front of them. This is still happening today. Many churches and believers reject the supernatural move of the Holy Spirit, including expressive worship, because it doesn't fit their theological framework. They would rather cling to tradition than experience transformation.

Breaking Free from a Religious Spirit: Living from the Revelation of Grace.

1. Repent from Legalism and False Religiosity

- ❖ Repent on behalf of yourself and your ancestral line for trusting in rituals rather than the Holy Spirit.
- ❖ Embrace the truth that righteousness comes through faith in Jesus, not religious performance.
- ❖ Let go of a judgmental mindset and cultivate a heart of grace.

2. Walk in True Humility

a) Begin Each Day with a Surrendered Prayer

Start your day by humbly acknowledging your dependence on God. Pray something like, "Lord, I can't do this without you. I surrender my plans, my strengths, and my weaknesses to you. Lead me today." This positions your heart to receive grace instead of trying to earn it through your own strength.

b) Resist the Urge to Perform for God

Reject the mindset that you need to "earn" God's love or favor. Stop striving to look holy on the outside while feeling empty inside. You can even take some time off serving God while you ask him to correct your mindset. I did this in my journey, and God honored it. Remember: God's grace is a gift, not a reward (Ephesians 2:8–9).

Replace performance with presence; create time to just be with God when you may be tempted to pick up some work at church.

c) Serve in Hidden Places. Look for opportunities to serve where no one sees or applauds.

❖ Clean, help, or give without announcing it.

❖ True humility is developed in secret.

d) Celebrate Others' Victories Without Comparison. When someone else gets blessed, healed, promoted, or delivered, celebrate them sincerely.

 ❖ Don't ask, "Why not me?" Instead, say, "Praise God for them!"

 ❖ This breaks jealousy and invites tangible manifestations of God's grace manifesting through unmerited favorable situations in your life.

3. Let Grace Free You from Striving

a) Shift Your Language from "I Have to" to "Jesus Already Did."

 ❖ Instead of saying, "I need to pray more so I can get free," say, "Because of what Jesus did, I have access to freedom through prayer."

 ❖ Remind yourself daily: "It is finished" (John 19:30).

b) Use Spiritual Disciplines to Connect, Not to Earn

 ❖ Fast, pray, and worship but not to earn deliverance but to connect with the Deliverer.

 ❖ These are tools to receive grace, not wages to earn favor.

Think: "I fast because I want to draw near, not because I'm trying to prove myself worthy of what I need from God."

c) Rest When You're Tempted to Strive

❖ When you feel overwhelmed trying to "do enough," pause.

❖ Take a deep breath, pray:

"Jesus, I rest in Your finished work. I receive Your grace today." Remember, "It is God who works in you to will and to act in order to fulfill his good purpose" (Philippians 2:13).

❖ Remind your soul as often as you can that freedom is a gift, not a paycheck.

4. Seek Deliverance Through Prayer and Spiritual Authority

Deliverance often requires partnering with trusted spiritual leaders who understand spiritual warfare.

❖ Have a mature believer or pastor pray for your deliverance.

❖ Engage in deep personal intercession, calling on the name of Jesus.

❖ Reject every lie the enemy has planted in your mind and replace it with the truth of God's Word.

5. Walk in the Holy Spirit's Guidance

Once free, stay free! The religious spirit wants to pull you back into performance-based Christianity, and the spirit spouse seeks to return through compromise.

❖ Stay rooted in God's Word and allow the Holy Spirit to lead your daily walk.

❖ Avoid old patterns, religious habits, and associations that fuel bondage.

Embrace intimacy with Christ rather than routine religion. Ask God to lead you on how and when to engage in Christian disciplines. Do not decide on how long to fast and when to fast on your own. Break a fast if you are on your period and you feel weak. Break a fast to celebrate a birthday or graduation and then go back to your fast. Grace allows for flexibility.

THE KEY OF
WARFARE

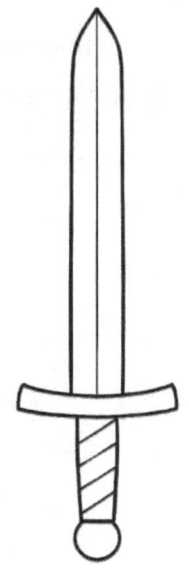

Color in: Green

CHAPTER 9

THE KEY OF WARFARE

My Testimony: Commanding, Not Begging

There is a realm in prayer where the believer stops pleading and begins to command. This is a place where spiritual warfare is not just reactionary but intentional, prophetic, and victorious. You can boldly stand in this place when you have received God's love. You respond with joy; you are living a life of worship; you have accepted His grace, and you extend it to others.

In the context of spiritual warfare, believers are encouraged to approach prayer like a courtroom, viewing God as the Judge, Jesus as their Advocate, and the Bible as the legal document affirming their freedom from spirit spouses. I didn't always know this. For a long time, my nights were tormented by a spirit spouse. I would wake up trembling, caught between exhaustion and fear. In those dark hours, I felt powerless. I cried. I begged. I pleaded with God to intervene. I sought help from every direction, going from one minister to another, hoping that someone could pray me into freedom, but I found no one.

God, in His kindness, opened my eyes, not to a new prophet or another pastor, but to the truth of who I was in Christ. He took me to Ephesians 2:6, "And God raised us up with Christ and seated us with him in the heavenly realms in Christ Jesus."

At that moment, I realized I was not a victim waiting for rescue. I was already seated with Christ, above the oppression and above the lies of the enemy. The chains were psychological, formed by fear and ignorance. I was not just saved; I was armed. Jesus had already declared in Luke 10:19, "I have given you authority to trample on snakes and scorpions and to overcome all the power of the enemy; nothing will harm you." That was my turning point.

I stopped praying like a beggar and started praying like a daughter of the King. I stood up in the middle of the night, looked into the invisible realm, and said, "Enough!" My voice shook not because I was scared, but because authority was waking up inside me. I wasn't asking the spirits to leave; I was commanding them to go. This is the essence of spiritual warfare: not screaming louder but standing taller in your divine identity.

You see, warfare prayer is not about emotional pleading. It's about legal enforcement. Heaven has already ruled in your favor; your job is to execute the verdict.

"What you decide on will be done, and light will shine on your ways" (Job 22:28).

When I embraced this, everything began to change. The atmosphere in my house shifted. My dreams were no longer battlegrounds; they became places of revelation. The torment broke because I had learned to command in faith, not cry in fear. I began to see what Paul meant when he said: "The weapons we fight with are not the weapons of the world. On the contrary, they have divine power to demolish strongholds" (2 Corinthians 10:4).

Practical Tools for Warfare: Engaging More Divine Weapons

God has provided us with powerful tools to actively engage the forces that oppose us. These tools are gifts from Heaven, each uniquely suited to deepen our connection with God and fortify us against any spirit, stronghold, or oppression. These weapons are accessible to every believer and they become increasingly powerful as our relationship with Christ grows.

The Armor of God

Ephesians 6:10-12, "Finally, be strong in the Lord and in his mighty power. Put on the full armor of God, so that you can take your stand against the devil's schemes. For our struggle is not against flesh and blood, but against the rulers, against the authorities, against the powers of this dark world and against the spiritual forces of evil in the heavenly realms."

In the realm of spiritual warfare, the imagery of the armor of God found in Ephesians 6 serves as a powerful reminder of the spiritual resources available to every believer. Each piece of this divine armor is essential for standing firm against the attacks of the enemy, including the disruptive influence of spirit spouses. Let's explore each piece in detail and understand how they equip us for effective spiritual engagement.

1. Belt of Truth: The Foundation of Our Defense

The belt of truth is the first piece of armor mentioned, and it serves as the foundational element in our spiritual warfare. In ancient times, a soldier's belt would hold their tunic in place and secure their weapons. Similarly, the truth of God's Word grounds us, preventing us from being swayed by deception. When dealing with spirit spouses who seek to manipulate our perceptions, the truth acts as our first line of defense. Grounding ourselves in the Word of God not only protects us from the lies that these spiritual forces propagate but also helps us identify and renounce false narratives that infiltrate our thoughts. For instance, when spirit spouses whisper feelings of inadequacy, shame, or unworthiness, the belt of truth reminds us of verses like 1 Peter 2:9, which declares that we are a "chosen people, a royal priesthood." Embracing this identity allows us to dismantle the false narratives imposed by spiritual enemies.

2. Breastplate of Righteousness: Guarding Our Hearts

Next, we put on the breastplate of righteousness, which is vital for protecting our hearts, the core of our emotions, desires, and spiritual vitality. The breastplate is designed to cover the heart and vital organs, symbolizing the importance of guarding our emotional and spiritual well-being.

When we walk in integrity and purity, we shield ourselves from the accusations and condemnations that spirit spouses might throw our way. Righteousness in Christ is not about our performance; it's about our position as redeemed children of God. This breastplate allows us to stand firm against the attacks aimed at undermining our worth and value.

3. Shield of Faith: Our Defense Against Doubt

The shield of faith acts as our protective barrier against the doubts and fears that spirit spouses often amplify. The shield used in Roman times was large enough to cover the whole body, providing essential protection in battle. Spirit spouses can sow seeds of uncertainty and insecurity, attempting to weaken our trust in God's promises. By raising our shield of faith, we extinguish the fiery darts launched by the enemy, asserting our confidence in God's goodness and faithfulness.

4. Helmet of Salvation: Protecting Our Identity

The helmet of salvation plays a crucial role in safeguarding our minds. Just as a soldier's helmet protects their head from fatal blows, the helmet of salvation protects our thoughts and beliefs about our identity in Christ. Spirit spouses often attempt to cloud our minds with confusion and fear, leading us to question our salvation and worthiness. By wearing the helmet of salvation, we declare that we are secure in our relationship with God. For example, Ephesians 2:8-9 reminds us that we are saved by grace through faith, not by our works. This knowledge reassures us and fortifies our minds against the lies that spirit spouses might present, allowing us to confidently reject any thoughts of unworthiness or insecurity.

5. Sword of the Spirit: Our Offensive Weapon

The sword of the Spirit, which is the Word of God, is our primary offensive weapon in spiritual warfare. Unlike the other pieces of armor that primarily serve as protection, the sword allows us to take the fight to the enemy. When we declare Scripture in the face of spiritual opposition, we wield the authority and power of God's truth. This sword allows us to cut through deception, exposing the lies propagated by spirit spouses. Jesus Himself demonstrated the power of Scripture during His temptation in the wilderness, responding to the enemy with specific verses that affirmed His identity and mission. By immersing ourselves in God's Word and learning to apply it in battle, we become equipped to confront the challenges posed by spiritual forces.

6. Shoes of Peace: Prepared for Battle

Finally, the shoes of peace prepare us to advance boldly in the Gospel. In Roman times, soldiers wore sandals with thick soles designed for stability and protection. The peace of God acts as our foundation, grounding us and enabling us to navigate spiritual battles without fear.

When confronted by the chaos that spirit spouses can bring into our lives, the peace of Christ steadies us. Philippians 4:7

assures us that "the peace of God, which transcends all understanding, will guard your hearts and your minds in Christ Jesus." With our shoes firmly planted, we can step forward in confidence, knowing that we carry the message of hope and reconciliation wherever we go. This peace allows us to face spiritual battles with a calm assurance that God is in control, and it compels us to share the Gospel, advancing God's Kingdom even in the face of opposition.

Praying the Armor: I recommend you do this daily to defeat the spirit spouse:

Upon myself, I put on the full armor of God

I put on the helmet of my salvation

The breastplate of righteousness

The shield of faith

The sword of the spirit

The belt of truth

The shoes of the gospel of peace

I declare and decree that I am fully armored in the spirit realm. If the devil comes at me one way, he will flee from me 7 different ways, according to Deuteronomy 28:7.

Midnight Prayer

My Testimony

There was a season in my life when I dreaded the night. I would fall asleep and find myself in an alternate universe, having nightmares that felt so real over and over again. Sexual dreams where demonic entities would masquerade as familiar pastors, friends, or even my children; dreams of forcefully eating against my will; dreams with gunmen chasing me with machetes; dreams of cleaning and cooking and working as a housemaid; dreams of going to old classrooms and struggling through tests, which would lead to intense fear in the dream, which in turn would lead to a strange orgasm, which would wake me up feeling like I was dying. I would wake up exhausted, ashamed, and confused. I thought they were "just dreams" until I realized that these dreams consistently signaled seasons of severe hardships in my physical life. I came to understand that God was allowing these dreams to show me that my destiny was being attacked, manipulated, and bound while I slept. That's when the Holy Spirit arrested me. He said, "Rise and fight back."

I began waking up consistently between the hours of midnight and 4 a.m. It was hard at first. My flesh resisted. The bed felt warm, but my spirit was tired of defeat. So, I rose. And what happened in those hours changed my life forever. I cried. I shouted. I prayed in tongues until sweat dripped from my face. I called on the blood of Jesus to wash me, and I renounced every evil covenant made knowingly or unknowingly. I broke spiritual marriages. I burned demonic contracts in the fire of the Holy Spirit. I was Holy Spirit possessed; I heard myself shouting out Scripture. It was like the same out-of-body feeling the spirit spouse used to bring upon me in moments of its torment, but this time, the Holy Spirit was in control of my person. I declared, "I belong to Jesus. My body is the temple of the Holy Spirit. My dreams are sanctified. My soul is not for rent!" At those moments, demons growled and screamed out of me, some of them shrieking as they left. I was coughing and burping and had to continuously rush to the bathroom. Jesus Himself was on the matter, and I was being set free. Sometimes, I would get so dizzy my husband would have to continue commanding and praying. And something shifted. The dreams stopped. The heaviness lifted. My life began to align with the will of God. There is now a new spirit in charge of my midnight hours because God gave me the grace to sacrifice those hours in prayer.

Midnight prayer is not just about the time on the clock; it is a spiritual realm, a portal of divine transaction, judgment, and breakthrough. It is where angels are dispatched, mysteries are revealed, and demonic systems are dismantled. The realm of midnight is not for the spiritually lazy. It is for the warrior. The one who has been denied for too long and is ready to take it by force. In nature, midnight marks a new day. In the spirit, midnight opens a gate. A gate into the courts of Heaven or a gate into demonic activity, depending on who shows up. The Lord gave us this strategy in His Word. Again and again, midnight was the hour of divine encounter and deliverance.

- ❖ Paul and Silas didn't wait for the morning. They sang and prayed at midnight, and Heaven responded with an earthquake.
- ❖ Boaz discovered Ruth at midnight, the hour of divine recognition and favor.
- ❖ The cry for the bridegroom in the parable of the ten virgins came at midnight, the hour of divine visitation.
- ❖ The firstborns of Egypt died at midnight, the hour of judgment and deliverance.

The Protocols of Midnight Warfare

Here's how to engage:

Set the Alarm: Discipline yourself. Set time aside between 12:00 a.m. and 4:00 a.m. After some time, the Holy Spirit will begin to wake you up Himself, and you will not need your alarm. He will pick the time He wants. In my case, He picked a specific time consistently.

Repent Deeply: Sin gives the enemy access. Purify your altar.

Engage in Thanksgiving: Bring to your mind the things you take for granted daily and thank God for them. Praise opens portals and invites angelic presence.

Enter the Courts: Take your case before God, quote Scriptures and call on His promises.

Declare and Decree: Speak life, break covenants, destroy soul ties and cancel spiritual marriages.

Pray in Tongues: Let the Spirit pray mysteries through you.

Anoint Yourself: Oil your head with oil that has been prayed over and blessed by yourself or a trusted and ordained spiritual leader. Call on the blood of Jesus by saying, "I cover myself with the blood of Jesus."

The Weapon of Prophetic Voices

In a world full of uncertainty, people often search for truth and direction in the wrong places, turning to astrology, crystals, and other spiritual trends that promise insight but ultimately lead away from God. This deep longing for spiritual guidance was never meant to be satisfied by the world, but by God Himself. Throughout Scripture, God makes His will known through prophets, His messengers who speak truth, offer direction, and reveal His plans. As Amos 3:7 says, "Surely the Sovereign LORD does nothing without revealing his plan to his servants the prophets."

Even today, prophetic voices are just as vital. Though often overlooked in a culture driven by science and secularism, God still speaks through those He appoints. True prophets aren't led by fame or gain, but by love for God and His people. When we honor the prophetic, we open ourselves to His clarity, peace, and purpose (2 Chronicles 20:20). Instead of following worldly trends, we can embrace the better way of hearing God through His Spirit and those He sends. Prophets have always helped God's people return to Him with hope, correction, and vision. Just as in Bible times, they still call us to walk in truth today.

Fasting

Fasting is not simply abstaining from food; it's a sacred practice of setting ourselves apart, creating a space where our spirits can more clearly connect with God. This act of devotion sharpens our spiritual sensitivity, enabling us to hear God's voice more distinctly and to discern the enemy's tactics more readily. In Matthew 17:21, Jesus teaches us that certain types of spiritual oppression cannot be broken except through prayer and fasting. This principle is especially potent in warfare, as fasting deepens our resilience and strengthens us to confront specific challenges.

When we fast, we humble ourselves before God, aligning our hearts with His purposes. Fasting clears away the distractions of daily life and brings us into a place of focus and surrender, making us more receptive to God's guidance. For those who struggle with the strongholds of a spirit spouse, fasting can be a critical step in weakening the enemy's hold, as it fortifies our spirits and invites God's power to dismantle spiritual entanglements.

The Power of Baptism in the Holy Spirit

As a believer, you've already taken that first bold step. You have accepted Jesus Christ into your life. You are born again, washed clean by the love of Jesus. But there's more waiting for you, something beautiful and soothing and empowering. It's the baptism in the Holy Spirit, a gift from Jesus Himself. This is a divine encounter that equips you to face the unseen enemies hiding in the corners of your life.

You see, being born again is like stepping into a new world, but the baptism in the Holy Spirit is like being handed a sword of light and a shield of fire. Jesus promised this gift, saying He would baptize us not just with water but with the Holy Spirit and with fire (Matthew 3:11).

My Story

I remember the first time I really leaned into praying in the Spirit. I'd lock myself away, sometimes for hours, just letting the Holy Ghost take over. Words I didn't understand spilled out of me: beautiful, powerful, and alive. It was like my spirit was waking up, stretching out, and growing stronger with every syllable. Tongues confuse the powers of darkness. They can't understand it or fight it. It's like throwing a blinding light into a room full of shadows; they scatter and run away. The more I prayed in tongues, the weaker that spirit spouse became. "For anyone who speaks in a tongue does not speak to people but to God. Indeed, no one understands them; they utter mysteries by the Spirit" (1 Corinthians 14:2).

Tongues aren't just for fighting battles; they're for building you up too. Every time you speak in the Spirit, it's like laying bricks in a tower that reaches toward God. Your faith grows, and your connection with the Father deepens. The Bible says it edifies you (1 Corinthians 14:4), which means it lifts you up, charges you up, and fills you with a strength you didn't know you had. When you're facing a spirit spouse or any other darkness, you need that strength.

Picture this: you're in your room, the world is quiet, and you start praying in tongues. At first, it might feel awkward, like you're stumbling over the words. But then the Holy Spirit takes the lead, and suddenly, it's flowing smoothly, strong, and unstoppable. An hour goes by, and you don't even notice. You're not just talking; you're waging war. You're tearing down strongholds, breaking chains, and sending every dark spirit running for the hills. And the best part is you are not doing it in your own power. The Holy Ghost is right there, giving you the utterance, guiding your voice, and filling you with His fire.

If you've already welcomed Jesus into your heart, don't stop there. Desire this gift. Ask for it with a hungry heart. Some Christians believe that when they have received Jesus in their hearts, they already have all of the Holy Spirit. Jesus promised He'd give the Holy Spirit to those who ask (Luke 11:13). If this is what you believe, then please consider reading about what is actually the truth found in Acts 8:5-8, 12-17. This Scripture lets us know that salvation and baptism in the Holy Spirit are two separate experiences.

If you have already received it, don't let it sit unused like a dusty old treasure chest. Open it up! Start with an hour a day speaking in tongues, letting the Holy Spirit move through you. Watch how your spirit comes alive, how your dreams get cleaner, and how your faith grows. The spirit spouse does not stand a chance against a believer filled with the Holy Spirit. This is your invitation to more. More power, more freedom, more of God. The baptism in the Holy Spirit isn't just a nice idea; it's a game-changer, a lifesaver, and a victory-maker.

The Sacraments as a Weapon of War

God instituted only two sacraments for believers. Baptism and communion. These are not only foundational to the Christian faith but also serve as powerful spiritual weapons in the context of warfare, especially in overcoming the influence of spirit spouses.

Communion also known as the Lord's Supper, is a practice observed to strengthen the believer's faith and fellowship with Christ. It is the eating of bread and wine, which, having been prayed over in thanksgiving memorial of Christ's death on the cross, have become symbols of his body and blood. Partaking in this represents the fact that as born-again Christians, we are under a new and more powerful covenant than any other covenant, including the spirit spouse covenant. "This cup is the new covenant in my blood, which is poured out for you" (Luke 22:20). Every time we take communion, we are brought back to the powerful, finished work of Christ on the cross, and we reaffirm our covenant with Christ as being superior to every other covenant. Through His death and resurrection, Jesus disarmed every power of darkness, securing victory for all who believe in Him. When we take communion, we reclaim this victory over every form of bondage, spiritual interference, or oppression that seeks to afflict us. We remember that the blood of Christ is our covering, a shield that no force of darkness can penetrate. For those struggling with a spirit spouse, communion serves as a reclaiming of our freedom, a reminder that no power, spirit, or stronghold; can stand against the blood of Jesus. If you are in a battle with the spirit spouse, I recommend that you make the practice of communion a daily habit. In our family, we have made it a practice to take communion every night when we do our bedtime prayers before bed.

Baptism is more than a symbolic ritual; it's a powerful spiritual weapon and a divine legal act that severs old covenants, including those formed through demonic ties like spirit spouses. Romans 6:3–4 declares that through baptism, we die to sin and rise into new life with Christ. It marks a break from the past and a step into our true identity in Him. Galatians 3:27

says, "For all of you who were baptized into Christ have clothed yourselves with Christ," signifying a spiritual covering that cancels prior ungodly attachments. I was baptized three times, the first as a teenager, forced (by narcissistic adults), and I was angry; the second, in defiance of the first, still lacking understanding. But the third time was different. In desperation for deliverance from a tormenting spirit spouse, I cried out to God. He asked me to be baptized again, not as a ritual, but as an act of worship grounded in sincere, biblical revelation. That third baptism marked a pivotal turning point in my journey to freedom. If you're battling spiritual bondage, especially in the form of a spirit spouse, I urge you to seek God, study His Word, and ask the Holy Spirit if baptism is the next step in your deliverance. Don't underestimate what God can do through this holy act of obedience.

Anointing

Anointing with oil is a powerful act of consecration, a declaration that we and our homes are set apart for God's purposes. In biblical times, anointing oil was used to mark prophets, priests, and kings, signifying that they were chosen and empowered by God. Today, we anoint ourselves, our families, and our living spaces as an act of spiritual protection, creating a boundary that declares, "This space belongs to God." When facing spiritual warfare, especially from forces as invasive as a spirit spouse, anointing becomes a shield, a tangible expression of our commitment to God. Anointing oil serves as a barrier against spiritual interference, marking our lives as holy and untouchable by the enemy. As we anoint ourselves, we invite the Holy Spirit to fill and empower us, breaking chains and surrounding us with His presence. Anointing is a reminder that we are under God's divine protection, safeguarded by His power, and dedicated to His purposes. If you are in a battle with spirit spouses, I recommend that you make it a practice to anoint yourself regularly in the name of Jesus. Pastors can make it a regular practice to have healing and anointing services at their churches.

Renouncing and Rebuking

Spirit spouses often operate under deceptive "agreements," claims, or bonds that can feel like a weight over the heart or mind. By the power of Jesus' name, we can break these agreements, severing their hold. Declare boldly, "In the name of Jesus, I renounce any connection or bond with this spirit spouse. I am a child of God, bought by the blood of Christ, and I reject any claim that spirit spouses attempt to have over my life." Speaking these words with conviction is a powerful act of defiance against the enemy. When you declare your identity in Christ and reject these false bonds, you weaken the power they once held over you.

Invoking the Blood of Jesus

The blood of Jesus is one of the most potent weapons in spiritual warfare. It's not only a reminder of Christ's sacrifice but also a shield against spiritual forces. When you declare, "I am covered by the blood of Jesus," you are setting a boundary that spirit spouses cannot cross. The blood acts as a protective shield in the spirit realm; you may not be able to see it, but Satan and his demons recognize it and flee. Hebrews 12:24, "You have come to Jesus the mediator of a new covenant, and to the sprinkled blood that speaks a better word than the blood of Abel." This shows that the blood of Jesus speaks, meaning it is active, visible, and has a voice in the spirit realm. So invoke the blood of Jesus over every aspect of your life: your mind, your heart, your relationships, and your home. Declare, "By the blood of Jesus, I am free from every bond, curse, and attachment. Spirit spouses have no power over me." There is divine power in proclaiming this truth, reminding the forces of darkness that they have been defeated by the sacrifice of Christ.

Hearing God's Voice

In the realm of spiritual warfare, divine strategy is essential. Throughout the Scriptures, we see a pattern of God providing specific instructions to His people, unique to them, during times of battle, illustrating that God desires to be actively involved in our struggles. For example, in 1 Samuel 30, we find David in a dire situation, having returned to find his city, Ziklag, burned and his families taken captive by the Amalekites. Instead of rushing into battle on his own, David sought the Lord for guidance, and God responded with a clear strategy for victory. This narrative underscores a vital principle: our battles are best fought when we align ourselves with God's plans.

In our own spiritual warfare, particularly when confronting the oppressive influences of spirit spouses, we must prioritize listening for God's voice. Engaging in spiritual warfare requires more than just knowledge; it demands an intimate relationship with God that is characterized by prayer, stillness, and a willingness to hear His instructions. Instead of relying solely on our understanding or experience, we allow the Holy Spirit to lead us, granting us insights that can be pivotal in our fight against the enemy.

Listening for divine strategies also requires an openness to the unexpected. God often works in ways that transcend our understanding, and His plans may not always align with our expectations. Just as He instructed David to pursue the Amalekites and assured him of victory, God may lead us to take steps that seem unconventional or challenging. It is essential to approach these moments with faith, trusting that God knows the best path to our victory.

Breaking Vows

Many believers walk in unnecessary bondage, not realizing the silent agreements they've made with the kingdom of darkness, disguised as vows. Vows can open the door to spiritual oppression, especially from spirit spouses, and must be dealt with if we are to walk in full deliverance and intimacy with God. What is a Vow? A vow is a solemn promise or assertion, often made with strong emotional conviction. It can be spoken in a moment of pain, bitterness, anger, or disappointment. But what we fail to realize is that in the spiritual realm, words are binding. Heaven and hell both record what we say, and the enemy is a legalist; he capitalizes on every careless or intentional vow we make. Proverbs 18:21, "The tongue has the power of life and death, and those who love it will eat its fruit." This lets us know that the words we speak bear fruits that show up as visible results. Below are some common examples of vows:

- ❖ "I will never trust a man again."
- ❖ "I don't need anyone in my life."
- ❖ "If this is what marriage is, I'd rather stay single forever."
- ❖ "I am always sick"

What feels like emotional venting becomes a contract in the spirit, a contract that often invites spirit spouses. Vows Are Absolutes and God Is Not in Them. When you say, "I will never…" or "I will always…," you enter the territory of absolutes. The danger here is this: only God is absolute. When you make yourself the final authority over your life, even unknowingly, you dethrone God and enthrone yourself. That is a subtle form of idolatry. God alone holds the future. When we vow in absolutes, we essentially say: "God, I don't trust you to write my story. I will write it myself." This rebellion, though unconscious, is a sin that must be repented of. In such cases, vows become more than just wrong thinking; they become altars that empower demonic spirits. For Example: You say, "I don't want a man in my life ever again. "The spirit spouse hears, "She's given me permission to take the place of any man in her life." Suddenly, godly relationships never work

263

out. You feel married in your dreams and suffer from rejection, barrenness, or unexplained illnesses.

The Danger of Hasty Emotional Promises: Sometimes vows aren't made out of fear or anger, but from false devotion. "God, if you give me this job, I'll never sin again." "If you give me a spouse, I'll fast every week." God doesn't want manipulative deals. He desires surrender. In Judges 11:29–40, Jephthah made a vow to sacrifice the first thing that came out of his house if God gave him victory. God did give him victory and the first thing that came out of his house… it was his daughter. His emotional, unnecessary vow cost him dearly. False promises are still vows, and the spirit spouse can take advantage of them to continue to torment its victims.

Breaking Vows and Closing Doors

Deliverance starts with revelation: Ask the Holy Spirit to reveal:

- ❖ Any vows you've made knowingly or unknowingly
- ❖ Vows made in childhood
- ❖ Vows spoken in trauma or heartbreak
- ❖ Ancestral vows made on your behalf through covenants, witchcraft, or tradition

Prayer for Breaking Vows

Heavenly Father, in the name of Jesus Christ, I repent for every vow I have made that contradicts your will for my life. I renounce every inner vow, every promise, every declaration I have spoken that gave the enemy legal ground in my life. I break these vows now by the power of the blood of Jesus. I nullify any ancestral vows made on my behalf through family, rituals, or bloodlines. I command every spirit, spouse, and demonic force attached to those vows to leave my life now! I am not in covenant with darkness; I am in covenant with the blood of Jesus Christ. I declare freedom, restoration, and divine alignment in Jesus' mighty name. Amen.

God's covenant is higher than any vow you or your ancestors have made. When we break ungodly vows, we step out of self-lordship and into the lordship of Jesus. We break the chains of the past and align with the purposes of Heaven.

THE KEY OF FAITH

Color in: Orange

CHAPTER 10

THE KEY OF FAITH

"Now faith is the substance of things hoped for, the evidence of things not seen" (Hebrews 11:1).

In the face of the challenges posed by spirit spouses, unwavering faith in God's promises becomes a source of strength, guarding our hearts and minds against the attacks of fear and doubt. These spiritual forces can create an atmosphere of confusion and despair, seeking to undermine our identity and purpose in Christ. However, the writer of Hebrews encourages us in Hebrews 10:23 to "hold fast the confession of our hope without wavering, for He who promised is faithful." This truth serves as a solid foundation upon which we can build our lives during the tumultuous journey of deliverance.

How To Activate the Key of Faith

1. The Word of God:

Hearing the Word is the Foundation of Faith. As Romans 10:17 says, "Consequently, faith comes from hearing the message, and the message is heard through the word about Christ." Faith grows when we immerse ourselves in Scripture. The Word of God is not just information; it's transformation. It fills us, shapes us, and bears the fruit of the Holy Spirit within us.

My Testimony

Let me share a breakthrough moment in my own journey of deliverance from the spirit spouse. Anyone who's faced this battle knows the torment of those disturbing sexual dreams so vivid they leave you feeling both violated and confused by the pleasure your body feels. One day, in desperation, I cried out to God and He responded with a question that pierced my soul:

"Sharon, you hate when the spirit spouse puts itself in you during the night, yet you recite Isaiah 54:5, 'Your Maker is your Husband,' but you haven't let me fully enter you. You only have bits and pieces of me inside you. You haven't read My Word from Genesis to Revelation."

I wept in deep repentance and deliverance. At that moment, I finally understood. Reading the Word wasn't just a discipline; it was intimacy. It was consummation. John 1:1 says, "In the beginning was the Word, and the Word was with God, and the Word was God." The Word is God. And when we haven't allowed the fullness of the Word into us, we leave ourselves spiritually vulnerable. The spirit spouse scans our soul to see if we've truly consummated our relationship with Christ. If we only have fragments of the Word, half-truths, and random verses, it gives the enemy legal ground to continue tormenting us. God showed me that just like a wife can't bear the full fruit of union with her husband through mere touching or petting, I couldn't bear the full fruit of the Spirit without fully receiving His Word. Reading the whole Bible, from Genesis to Revelation, is part of spiritually receiving my Bridegroom.

Before this revelation under the key of Faith, the spirit spouse fought hard to keep me from reading the Bible. I'd feel dizzy. The letters would blur. I'd give up. I only read random passages, but never the whole counsel of God. But in His mercy, the Lord set me free. He said, "This first time, don't worry about understanding everything. Just let me in. Get the whole Word in you. Later, come back and go deeper." So, I read; this time powered by revelation and the desire to be intimate with God, no longer from religion. The attacks against be reading lost their power. I was hungry like a starving soul tasting real food for the first time. Just as a married couple must continue meeting intimately for their union to flourish, so must we allow Jesus, the Living Word, to regularly enter us. Not once but again and again. Intimacy with Him must be cultivated.

If you haven't read the whole Bible yet, I urge you to start today. Set aside time daily. Let Jesus fully enter you through His Word so that when the spirit realm scans you, it sees the evidence of your covenant. You are not available. You are already spoken for. Then, return and study it again slowly, prayerfully. Let it take root. Immerse yourself. Read aloud, listen to Scripture audibly, and join a Bible group. As you do, your faith will grow, your intimacy with Christ will deepen, and the grip of the spirit spouse will be broken once and for all.

2. Active Imagination:

Another practical way to activate the key of faith is by engaging in active imagination, a spiritual discipline where your sanctified imagination aligns with the Word of God. It is the same tool God gave Abraham when He told him to count the stars and imagine his descendants. God often speaks through pictures, visions, and faith-filled thoughts to shape our reality. If you are believing God for marriage, watch wedding videos and imagine yourself getting married too. Close your eyes and see yourself as God sees you. Holy, pure, and covered in the blood of Jesus. Imagine chains falling off, wedding rings from counterfeit spirits being thrown into the fire, and a heavenly covering replacing all illegal covenants. Faith begins with seeing what God sees.

-Picture the Presence of God Driving out Darkness: Visualize the light of God entering every dark area of your soul. Where the spiritual spouse once had access, imagine Jesus standing guard, declaring, "This one is mine." The light overcomes the darkness every time (John 1:5).

-Imagine the Promise Fulfilled: Faith brings God's promises into the now. Imagine yourself walking in divine wholeness, in healthy relationships, free from tormenting dreams or emotional attachments to the past.

3. Make Faith Declarations:

Declare What You See in the Spirit. Your words are powerful. What you imagine by faith, speak aloud. "I cancel every demonic marriage by the authority of Jesus. I receive the covenant of Christ. I am free, pure, and whole." Faith grows when spoken.

4. Keep the Vision Before You:

Just like God told Habakkuk to write the vision, keep your faith image alive. Write out the future you see in your mind's eye without the spirit spouse. Revisit it daily. Faith is sustained through repetition and alignment with truth.

5. Step Out of Your Comfort Zone:

Take the leap of faith. Faith means trusting God enough to move, even when you don't have all the details. Sometimes, when you step into this place of divine imagination, God will show you something that feels big or unfamiliar. That's your invitation to step out of your comfort zone. When you use godly imagination, you're not just dreaming; you're beginning to see what God sees. Don't stay stuck because it feels safe. Faith grows when you take that first step. God will give you what it takes to match your obedience. Faith is not fantasy; it is the God-given ability to see what He sees and agree with it until it manifests. When used against spiritual spouses, faith becomes a fire that burns every ungodly tie and a sword that enforces your freedom in Christ.

THE KEY OF FREEDOM

Color in: Purple

CHAPTER 11

KEY OF FREEDOM

We don't fight for freedom. We fight from freedom.

These Scriptures reveal that freedom is not a future promise; it's a current reality for those who are in Christ. The enemy's goal is to deceive us into believing we are still bound. But the truth is that Jesus already defeated Satan and his demons at the cross. Our job is to enforce that victory by walking in revelation. "It is for freedom that Christ has set us free. Stand firm, then, and do not let yourselves be burdened again by a yoke of slavery" (Galatians 5:1).

What Does It Mean?

Revelation knowledge is different from head knowledge. It's not just knowing something in your mind; it's when truth becomes real and alive in your spirit. When you walk in the revelation that you are already free, it changes the way you think, pray, and fight. It shifts you from begging God to deliver you; to declaring the freedom He already gave you.

The Power of Surrender: Finding True Freedom in Christ

True freedom isn't found in control but in surrendering fully to Jesus. The world offers false freedom rooted in self, but Christ invites us to lay down our pride, sin, and fears to receive healing, peace, and purpose. Submission to Christ is not losing identity but discovering it. It's a journey of letting go of what binds us, like pornography, overeating, witchcraft, fear, control and people pleasing, and embracing the joy of obedience, repentance, and trust in God's rule.

My surrender came when God called me to leave my nursing career and stay home to care for my children, who were facing health issues at that time. It was hard, misunderstood, and financially risky. But in obedience, I saw deliverance for myself and my family. True freedom cost me my career, my identity as a nurse, and worldly security. But I gained far more: healing, purpose, and a spiritually grounded family. Not everyone will be called to leave their profession to follow God's call. Each journey with Him is unique. But one truth remains: true freedom in Jesus will always come with a cost. For some, it may mean devoting more intentional time to prayer and seeking deeper intimacy with Him. For others, it could be a call to prioritize family over personal ambitions, to resolve deep-rooted issues, or to step away from relationships and patterns that hinder spiritual growth. Jesus requires us to surrender anything that competes with His place in our lives. The process of letting go may feel challenging, but it's in this surrender that we encounter the profound, unshakeable freedom Jesus promises.

Freedom is the final key because it is evidence that the other six keys have done their work. Without receiving God's love, we cannot truly love others. Without love, joy becomes fleeting, worship becomes performance, grace becomes hard to give, warfare becomes exhausting, and faith becomes unstable. But when love takes root, joy overflows, worship rises, grace flows freely, warfare is victorious, and faith becomes unshakable. That's when freedom shows up not just as a feeling, but as the way we actually live.

Chapter 12

BEYOND DELIVERANCE

Pursuing a Relationship with Christ

Dear reader,

I want to remind you again of who you are in Christ: deeply loved, fully known, and already victorious. You may still face battles, but you do so from a position of victory, not defeat. My prayer is that these final reflections will inspire you to pursue not just what God can do for you, but who He is. When your heart is set on Him, everything else begins to fall into place.

As you read through this book, you would have observed by now that my struggle with the spirit spouse was a journey I would never have chosen, one filled with heartbreak, confusion, and countless sleepless nights. Desperation became my constant companion, but so did determination. I refused to accept defeat. I threw myself into every spiritual practice I could think of: praying with fervor, fasting until I was sick, and partaking in Holy Communion without revelation, believing each action would somehow break the chains. I visited countless men and women of God, chasing the hope that someone, somewhere, had the key to my freedom. Church after church, altar call after altar call, I pleaded for deliverance. I lived in a cycle of relentless striving, clinging to the belief that my efforts would eventually tip the scales in my favor. But the harder I tried, the more elusive freedom became.

My prayers seemed to bounce off the ceiling. My fasting felt like an empty ritual. The men and women of God I sought out were kind and sincere, but their prayers left me with short-lasting relief. As days turned into weeks and weeks into years, I started to wonder, Why isn't this working? What am I doing wrong? God's whisper began to rise in the back of my mind. He said, "There's something you're missing. You're chasing the wrong thing." At first, I didn't understand. I thought, What could be more important than deliverance? Wasn't that what I was supposed to be asking for? But the more I prayed, the more this truth became clear: I was seeking the gift of deliverance, but I wasn't seeking the Giver. I was pursuing the works of God's hands, but I wasn't pursuing His heart.

This realization hit me like a ton of bricks. I had spent years desperately looking for someone who could "fix" me. My prayers were filled with petitions, my fasts fueled by a singular desire: Lord, take this away from me. But the truth was, I didn't truly want Him. I wanted what He could do for me. This was a painful awakening. I had spent so much energy striving for deliverance that I had missed the most important thing: the freedom that comes from simply being in love with God. My problem wasn't my prayers or my fasting; it was the posture of my heart.

The turning point came when I stopped striving and started surrendering. I let go of the mindset that said, if I just do this, God will finally move. Instead of chasing after freedom, I began chasing after Him. My prayers changed. They weren't filled with frantic cries of "Lord, deliver me!" Instead, I found myself saying, "Lord, I love you. Help me to know you more. Help me to trust you, even in this." This wasn't an overnight change. It was a gradual process of unlearning old habits and replacing them with a deeper hunger for God's presence. Instead of spending hours strategizing my next spiritual move, like what prayer to pray or what fast to attempt, I began spending time simply being with Him. It was in this place that the 7 key concepts were born.

I believe many of the pastors who prayed for me were truly casting out demons. Deliverance was happening, but I kept losing it. What I didn't understand at the time and what many don't realize is that casting a demon out is only the beginning of deliverance and not the completion. Jesus Himself warned us in Matthew 12:43–45, "When an impure spirit comes out of a person, it goes through arid places seeking rest and does not find it. Then it says, 'I will return to the house I left.' When it arrives, it finds the house unoccupied, swept clean and put in order. Then it goes and takes with it seven other spirits more wicked than itself, and they go in and live there. And the final condition of that person is worse than the first. That is how it will be with this wicked generation."

This Scripture makes it clear that freedom that isn't followed by spiritual filling and transformation through a life built on intimacy with Christ is vulnerable to being translated into worse bondage.

Pastors and ministers are good, but it is essential that you become equipped yourself because when the demons come back, there might not be a pastor there at that second to help you drive them away. Each key represents a biblical principle that doesn't just set you free; it keeps you free:

Love heals your identity.

Joy fills your soul with strength.

Worship brings God's presence.

Grace replaces shame and striving.

Warfare equips you to fight back.

Faith anchors you in truth.

Freedom becomes your new lifestyle.

What I learned in that season changed me forever. I realized that true deliverance isn't just about the absence of struggle; it's about the presence of God. It's not about being free from every battle, but about knowing that, even in the battle, He is with you, sustaining you, and holding you close. This revelation brought me back to one of the most profound moments in Scripture, which is the night Jesus prayed in the Garden of Gethsemane. It's a scene that most believers are familiar with, but for me, it took on a new depth as I reflected on my own struggles. In the garden, Jesus, the Son of God, fully divine yet fully human, knelt alone. He was fully aware of what was coming: betrayal by a close friend, public disgrace, unimaginable physical suffering, and the crushing weight of humanity's sin. But beyond the pain of the cross itself, He faced something even greater: separation from the Father as He became the sacrifice for our sins. And in that moment, Jesus poured out His heart to the Father. He was honest, vulnerable, and transparent. He prayed, "Father, if it is possible, let this cup pass from me." He wasn't pretending to be okay with what was coming. He didn't hide His anguish. He admitted the pain and dread He felt at the thought of drinking that bitter cup. But here's the part that changed everything for me: Jesus didn't make His will the final word. Instead, He said, "Nevertheless, not my will, but yours be done."

I realized how often my own prayers had been filled with cries for deliverance without a deeper desire for God's will. I wanted freedom from my pain, but did I want His will above all else? Did I trust Him enough to say, "Not my will, but yours be done"? As I reflect on this now, I realize in those dark hours, God was forming me like a sharpened arrow (Isaiah 49:2). He was creating this book you are holding; He was laying the foundation for the Spirit Spouse Deliverance Prayer Room I host, He was birthing Worship War Win sessions, and He was forming a women's minister for New Day Christian Church. He was creating content for the dear souls who follow my social media and who find encouragement and a path to Christ in the light of my own journey. I saw darkness and doom; God saw a ministry baby growing in a womb, which needed time. He was downloading blueprints and showing me where deliverance keys are hidden so that I could strengthen my brethren after I had overcome (Luke 22:32). This journey taught me that Jesus Christ is not just the answer to my problems; He is the reward for all my godly endeavors. To anyone still in the middle of the struggle, let me encourage you with this: Freedom isn't proven by the absence of sexual dreams; it's proven by what you do when they come. There was a time when I'd have these dreams and spiral, crying, confused, yet still walking right into the very thing God was trying to warn me about. I'd go on to invite the wrong person in, make the wrong choice, and end up trapped in another painful cycle. That was bondage. Now, I am no longer experiencing oppressive sexual dreams that lead to continuous pain cycles.

So I tell you this: if a dream comes, don't let it paralyze you; let it instruct you. The Lord is allowing it to uncover a hidden motive or a subtle idol, and you have the power to respond in obedience. That's freedom. Not the lack of warfare, but the clarity to recognize it, the authority to stop it, and the courage to choose God's way. The secret to true freedom isn't in the actions you take; it's in the intimacy you cultivate with Christ. After you have cultivated intimacy with Christ, He may ask you to take actions that will deliver you, but those actions will be birthed from a place of intimacy, not control. When you seek Him with all your heart, when you love Him for who He is and not just for what He can do, deliverance becomes a by-product of His presence.

Jesus Christ is not just able to deliver you; He wants to. But even more than your freedom, He wants your heart so he can transform it, to make you ready to live your eternity in his Kingdom. Let your prayer be, "Lord, even if you don't deliver me in the way I hope, I will still love you. You are my Deliverer, my Healer, my everything." So, walk forward in confidence. Not because you have it all figured out, but because you have Him. And with Him, you have the promise of eternal life. As you step into this new chapter of your life, remember this: you are not fighting alone. You are surrounded by the God Who sees (El Roi), the God Who parts seas, walks through fire, and breaks every chain, and who loves you so much that He sent His only Son, Jesus Christ, to die for you.

With Love from *Sharon Mbi*

A Personal Invitation to Know Jesus Christ

Life After Death Starts with a Choice

If you've been reading this book and you don't know Jesus Christ as your personal Lord and Savior. I want you to know this. There is life after death. One day, your body will die, but your soul will live forever. The question is: where?

Without Jesus, you will be separated from God forever. That place of separation is called hell, and it's real. It's not just for "bad people." It's where we all deserve to go because of sin. But God, in His love, made a way out for us all, and that way is His Son, Jesus Christ Jesus came to this earth, lived without sin, died on the cross for your sins, and rose again to give you eternal life. That means life after death with God and also life with purpose and peace while you're still here on earth. You cannot earn this life. You can't buy it, work for it, or be good enough to deserve it. You must receive it by faith.

"If you confess with your mouth, 'Jesus is Lord,' and believe in your heart that God raised Him from the dead, you will be saved" (Romans 10:9).

That's it. This is how you receive eternal life. If you don't make this choice, you remain spiritually lost no matter how much good you do or how spiritual you feel. But today, you

285

can change that. If you're ready to receive Jesus and start a new life, pray this from your heart:

"Lord Jesus, I believe you are the Son of God. I believe you died for my sins and rose again. Please forgive me. I confess that you are Lord. I give you my life. Come into my heart and save me. I receive your gift of eternal life. Help me live for you from this day on. In Jesus' name, Amen."

If you prayed that and meant it, Heaven is rejoicing. You now belong to Jesus, and your eternity is secure.

Welcome to your new life!

WARFARE PRAYERS & DECLA-RATIONS

Prayers to Defeat the Spirit Spouse

Lord Jesus, today I repent of the sin of idolatry practiced by me through my ancestors. I ask you to forgive me and my generational line for making covenants with demons through the worship of graven images. Please forgive me for the ancestral sin of depending on evil spirits through witch doctors, soothsayers, tarot card readers, and sangomas for direction and solutions to my problems.

Today, I renounce this sin and ask that you reveal all hidden idolatry within me, whether it be self-dependence, depending on other humans, and/or people-pleasing. Please forgive me, my children, and all future generations. According to Your Word in 1 John 1:9, I receive your forgiveness now in Jesus's name.

Lord Jesus, today I come before You to repent of all of my sexual sins as well as all generational sexual sins of masturbation, entertaining and enjoying spirit husband/wife visits, fornication, adultery, molestation of children, rape, petting, flirting, and/or kissing outside of marriage, homosexuality, lesbianism, and all forms of sexual impurity and perversion that may have been practiced by me or my ancestors and/or my spouse and their ancestors (if married). I renounce these sins and receive your cleansing and forgiveness through your blood.

I call up all the demons associated with all the above-mentioned sins and cast them out of my body, soul, emotions, environment, children, and home. I renounce them forever and command them to leave now and go to the pit of hell, never to return to me or any of my descendants ever again in Jesus' name.

I stand on the Word of God in Isaiah 54:5, which states that I am married to my Maker, Jesus Christ.

You demon, claiming me as your spouse, I renounce you and cast you out of my life in Jesus' name.

According to Colossians 1:13, I have been translated from the kingdom of darkness where the spirit spouse (incubus or succubus) resides, and I now belong to Jesus Christ's Kingdom; therefore, I cast you, spirit spouse, out of my life and destiny in Jesus' name.

I declare that, according to Revelation 5:9, I have been pur-chased back by the blood of Jesus Christ from every spirit spouse (incubus or succubus). Therefore, I nullify every bride price paid on my behalf by the spirit claiming me as its spouse through ancestral covenants or my own sin or my spouse's sin (if you are married) in Jesus' name.

I break every generational pact and covenant made with any demon claiming me as its spouse, and I declare that, according to Isaiah 49:25, I am completely set free from the stipulations that entered my life and destiny from these covenants or pacts in Jesus' name.

Dear Holy Spirit, take over my body, spirit, and soul accord-ing to 1st Corinthians 6:19; my body, my sexual organs, my sleep time, and my mind belong to you. I bind the demon claiming me as its spouse, and I LOOSE my body, my sexual organs, my sleep time, and my mind from its control and do-minion in Jesus' name.

Dear Holy Spirit, You are my helper and my friend. Please give me the revelation of the 7 keys that I have through Christ Jesus, which are Your LOVE, JOY, WORSHIP, GRACE, WARFARE, FAITH, and FREEDOM, so that I can use them to pull down all strongholds and close all doors in my life that have been opened to the spirit claiming me as its spouse.

Today, I release myself to be happily married to an earthly spouse, which represents my relationship with Christ as His bride, according to Ephesians 5:25, in Jesus' name.

Prayers to Defeat the Spirit Spouse Attached to Your Spouse

Lord Jesus, today I stand in the gap for my spouse, and I ask you to forgive them of all generational sins that may have covenanted them to an evil spirit.

Heavenly Father, I ask that you visit my spouse today and shine your light and power into them and convict them of their need for deliverance so that we can both be free from spirit spouses and have a marriage that glorifies you completely.

You spirit spouse attached to my spouse, your time is up! I stand today on behalf of my spouse. According to Mark 10:8-9, we are one; therefore, I command you to release them from your dominion and authority in Jesus' name.

By the power that raised Christ from the dead, I remove my spouse from the alternate universe you, spirit spouse, have created for them, where they are led to believe that you do not exist.

I command that their spiritual eyes be opened and their heart become sensitive to the prompting of the Holy Spirit so that they can be brought to the place where they themselves, by "their will," will renounce all pacts and covenants that have allowed a spirit spouse into our lives.

Until the time when my spouse will renounce their spirit spouse and we will become one under Christ, I stand in the place of intercession and ask for a covering over my children according to 1 Corinthians 7:14, which states that the unbelieving wife has been made holy through her believing husband. If that were not the case, your children would not be pure and "clean." But as it is, they are HOLY.

I bind and cast out and stop the works of the spirit claiming my spouse as theirs in our lives, especially over our children, finances, and health, in Jesus' name, amen.

I command circumstances and situations to align themselves, governed by the mercy and grace of Jesus Christ, for my spouse to come to the full realization of their need for deliverance and, in humility, seek complete freedom in Jesus' name. Please, Heavenly Father, when my spouse becomes ready for deliverance, lead us to the right places and people who will help bring forth this deliverance without shaming us.

Heavenly Father, please make me and my spouse one in spiritual warfare so we can fight together and operate with unity so that you may be glorified.

Heavenly Father, please help me to stay in the place of inter-cession, humility, joy, and patience as I wait for You to go to work in my spouse's heart so that all the above can be accom-plished and we as a family can experience complete victory in Jesus' mighty name. AMEN.

Prayers to Defeat Anxiety & Depression Caused by a Spirit Spouse

Heavenly Father, forgive me for believing and tolerating the spirit of fear. I renounce all unconscious and subconscious fears within me in Jesus' name and choose by my will to do the work that it takes to renew my mind with the Word of God and replace all fearful thoughts with faith in Jesus Christ.

I declare that I do not have a spirit of fear and depression, but that of power, love, and a sound mind.

You spirit of anxiety and depression; I cast you out of my life now in Jesus' name.

Heavenly Father, please reveal wrong thought patterns that open the door to anxiety and depression and show me how to overcome them in Jesus' name.

I break every ancestral covenant I may have with the spirit of fear, not loving myself, people-pleasing, depression, anxiety, mental illness, heaviness, and oppression in Jesus' name.

I declare that, according to 1 Corinthians 2:16, I have the mind of Christ.

I break free from continuous cycles of PTSD, depression, anxiety, and panic attacks in Jesus' name.

I command every demon responsible for giving me nightmares and unfortunate situations in order to strengthen the stronghold of the spirit of torment through nervous system dysregulation to leave my life now in Jesus' name.

I pull down every stronghold of depression and anxiety with the blood of JESUS Christ.

I close every evil door that has been opened by the spirit of fear and depression into my life, and I open every good door that has been closed by these spirits in Jesus' name.

I pray for supernatural healing for all diseases that have entered my body through the spirits of fear, such as hypertension, heart palpitations, migraine headaches, insomnia, dizziness, heaviness, spirits of infirmity, an overactive autonomic nervous system, and a failed parasympathetic nervous system. In Jesus' name, I receive my healing according to Isaiah 53:5 and Malachi 4:2.

I pray, Lord, that you would supernaturally heal my parasympathetic nervous system and show me practical ways to relax my body and love myself.

I cast out of my life all evil spirits associated with the spirits of fear, oppression, and depression. All their helper spirits like stress, trauma, worry, overthinking, rumination and obsessive compulsions must leave me now in Jesus' name.

Declarations for the Key of Love

1. Walking in Love, Not Fear

I decree and declare that I am walking in love and not in fear, for God's perfect love casts out all fear. 1 John 4:18 says, "There is no fear in love. But perfect love drives out fear, because fear has to do with punishment." I declare that my heart is open to receive and give love, free from fear, free from doubt, and free from condemnation. I am secure in God's perfect love for me, and I release every fear, knowing that I am fully known, fully accepted, and fully loved by Him.

2. Healed and Whole in God's Love

Lord, I declare that your love makes me whole. Psalm 147:3 says, "He heals the brokenhearted and binds up their wounds." Every wound, every heartbreak, and every hurt from my past is being healed in your love. I release all bitterness, resentment, and unforgiveness, and I receive the fullness of your healing love. My heart is whole, my spirit is strong, and I walk in complete healing through the love of Christ.

3. Overflowing with Love for Others

I decree that my heart overflows with love for others, empowered by the Holy Spirit. Romans 5:5 says, "...because God's love has been poured out into our hearts through the Holy Spirit, who has been given to us." I declare that as I receive God's love, it overflows from me to everyone I encounter. I am filled with compassion, kindness, and grace, and I see others through the lens of God's love. I reject all anger, resentment, or pride and embrace the love of God that compels me to forgive and show mercy.

4. Clothed in Love and Free from Judgment

Father, I declare that I am clothed in love, which binds everything together in perfect harmony. Colossians 3:14 says, "And over all these virtues put on love, which binds them all together in perfect unity." I reject any spirit of judgment, condemnation, or criticism, and I choose to walk in love, extending grace as you have shown me grace.

5. Receiving and Walking in God's Everlasting Love

Father, I declare that I am receiving and walking daily in your everlasting love. Jeremiah 31:3 says, "I have loved you with an everlasting love; I have drawn you with unfailing kindness." I accept your invitation to walk in a love that is eternal, unfailing, and unconditional. I declare that I will not settle for any counterfeit love or fear-based attachment, but I will remain fully embraced by your true and lasting love for my foundation, and my fulfillment.

Declarations for the Key of Joy

1. Joy as My Strength

I declare that the joy of the Lord is my strength. Nehemiah 8:10 says, "Do not grieve, for the joy of the Lord is your strength." I decree that every trace of heaviness and sorrow is replaced by God's strength and joy. I walk in joy that overcomes every trial and lifts me above every burden, for my strength comes not from circumstances but from the Lord Himself.

2. Joy from God's Presence

Father, I receive the fullness of joy that is found in your presence. Psalm 16:11 says, "You make known to me the path of life; you will fill me with joy in your presence, with eternal pleasures at your right hand." I decree that as I draw close to you, my heart is filled with abundant joy. Nothing can steal my joy, because it is rooted in the unchanging presence of my loving God.

3. Joy Amidst Every Trial

Lord, I declare that I will count it all joy, even in trials. James 1:2-3 says, "Consider it pure joy, my brothers and sisters, whenever you face trials of many kinds, because you know that the testing of your faith produces perseverance." I decree that no difficulty or challenge can take my joy, because I trust that you are working all things for my good. I am filled with joy, knowing that you are using each trial to strengthen my faith.

4. Joy as My Inheritance

I decree that joy is my inheritance as a child of God. Romans 15:13 says, "May the God of hope fill you with all joy and peace as you trust in Him, so that you may overflow with hope by the power of the Holy Spirit." I declare that I am filled with God's joy, which overflows within me, bringing hope to every situation. My joy is not circumstantial; it is rooted in the power of the Holy Spirit.

5. Joy That Overcomes Sorrow

Lord, I declare that you have turned my mourning into joy. Isaiah 61:3 says that you will give me "a crown of beauty instead of ashes, the oil of joy instead of mourning." I decree that every season of sorrow is behind me, and I step forward into your joy. I receive your healing and the oil of gladness, declaring that I am filled with joy instead of sorrow and beauty instead of despair.

Declarations for the Key of Worship

1. Wholehearted Worship

I decree that I will worship the Lord with all my heart, soul, mind, and strength. Psalm 103:1 says, "Praise the LORD, my soul; all my inmost being, praise his holy name." I declare that every part of me, my body, mind, and spirit, will lift up praises to God. My heart will exalt His name, my mind will meditate on His goodness, and my body will express His glory in every action. I worship Him with my entire being.

2. Worship in Spirit and Truth

I decree that I will worship the Father in spirit and in truth. John 4:24 says, "God is spirit, and His worshipers must worship in the Spirit and in truth." I declare that my worship is genuine, flowing from a heart surrendered to God. I lay down any falsehood, pride, or fear, coming before Him in humility, honesty, and reverence. May my worship be a pure offering pleasing to the Lord.

3. Worship as Warfare

I declare that my worship is a weapon of spiritual warfare. Psalm 149:6 says, "May the praise of God be in their mouths and a double-edged sword in their hands." I decree that as I lift up praises, the atmosphere around me shifts, and every work of darkness is defeated. I proclaim victory through worship, praise unleashes God's power over every obstacle, fear, and attack of the enemy.

4. Worship That Transcends Circumstances

I declare that my worship is not dependent on my circumstances. Philippians 4:4 says, "Rejoice in the Lord always. I will say it again: Rejoice!" I decree that I will worship God no matter what I face. Whether in times of joy or sorrow, victory or defeat, my worship will remain steadfast. I declare that my worship transcends circumstances because it is anchored in the unshakable love and faithfulness of God.

5. Worship as a Lifestyle

I declare that worship is not just a moment but a lifestyle. Colossians 3:17 says, "And whatever you do, whether in word or deed, do it all in the name of the Lord Jesus, giving thanks to God the Father through Him." I decree that every action I take, every word I speak, and every thought I entertain will be an act of worship to God. My life is a continual offering of praise and gratitude, reflecting His love, grace, and glory in all that I do.

Declarations for the Key of Grace

1. Grace Overcomes Every Stronghold

I decree that by the grace of God, every stronghold of the spirit spouse over my life is broken. 2 Corinthians 12:9 says, "But he said to me, "My grace is sufficient for you, for my power is made perfect in weakness." Therefore, I will boast all the more gladly of my weaknesses, so that the power of Christ may rest upon me." I declare that the grace of God is sufficient to tear down every stronghold the spirit spouse has built in my life. I am empowered to overcome all forces that seek to control me.

2. Grace for Spiritual Restoration

I declare that the grace of God restores all that has been stolen by the spirit spouse. Joel 2:25 says, "I will repay you for the years the locusts have eaten." I proclaim that the grace of God is at work in my life, bringing restoration in every area that has been affected by spiritual bondage. The spirit spouse's hold is broken, and I receive God's grace to restore my relationships, my joy, and my destiny.

3. Grace to Walk in Purity and Wholeness

I declare that the grace of God empowers me to walk in purity and wholeness, free from the destructive influence of spirit spouses. Titus 2:11-12 says, "For the grace of God has appeared that offers salvation to all people. It teaches us to say "No" to ungodliness and worldly passions, and to live self-controlled, upright and godly lives in this present age." I decree that by grace, I am walking in purity, saying "No" to any spirit spouse or demonic influence that seeks to contaminate my life. I am whole in Christ, and I live uprightly before Him.

4. Grace to Reclaim My Identity in Christ

I declare that the grace of God is securing my identity in Christ, and I am no longer bound by the false identity imposed by the spirit spouse. 1 Corinthians 5:17 says, "I am in Christ. I am a new creation. The old has passed away." I no longer live under the weight of my past. I walk in the new life God has given me, redeemed, restored, and free.

5. Grace for Emotional Healing

I declare that the grace of God is healing my heart and emotions from the wounds caused by the spirit spouse. Psalm 147:3 says, "He heals the brokenhearted and binds up their wounds." I decree that God's grace is restoring my emotional health and healing the wounds that have been inflicted by spiritual bondage. I walk in emotional freedom and wholeness, no longer burdened by the past.

Declarations for the Key of Warfare

1. Warfare to Reclaim My Peace and Joy

I decree that the spirit spouse and every demonic force trying to rob me of my peace and joy are bound in Jesus' name. Philippians 4:7 says, "And the peace of God, which transcends all understanding, will guard your hearts and your minds in Christ Jesus." I declare that peace is my portion, and the spirit spouse's attempts to steal my peace are rendered powerless. I declare that joy is my inheritance in Christ, and no spirit of torment will rob me of it again.

2. Warfare to Restore My Relationships

I declare war against every spirit spouse that has interfered with my relationships and my marriage. Matthew 18:18 says, "Truly I tell you, whatever you bind on earth will be bound in heaven, and whatever you loose on earth will be loosed in heaven." I bind the spirit spouse and every demonic force attempting to disrupt or destroy my relationships, and I loose healing, reconciliation, and peace in my relationships. The spirit spouse's influence is broken, and I walk in restoration and unity.

3. Warfare to Reclaim My Destiny

I declare that I am walking in the fullness of my divine destiny, free from every spirit spouse's influence. Jeremiah 29:11 says, "For I know the plans I have for you," declares the Lord, "plans to prosper you and not to harm you, plans to give you hope and a future." I declare that I will not be diverted or hindered from my divine purpose by any spirit spouse or demonic force. The plans of the Lord for my life will be fulfilled, and I reject any counterfeit that the enemy has tried to place in my path. I reclaim my future and my hope in Christ Jesus.

4. Warfare for Restoration of Family Lineage

I declare that every curse, demon, and spirit spouse operating through my family bloodline is broken and nullified by the power of the blood of Jesus. Exodus 20:5-6 says, "For I, the Lord your God, am a jealous God, punishing the children for the sin of the parents to the third and fourth generations of

those who hate Me, but showing love to a thousand generations of those who love Me and keep My commandments." I
declare that my family lineage is being restored and cleansed
by the blood of Jesus. Every generational curse of idolatry,
witchcraft, and occult practice is broken, and I claim freedom
for my descendants in the name of Jesus.

5. Warfare for Deliverance from Sexual Bondage

I declare that I am free from every sexual spirit spouse that has
been assigned to bind me in sexual torment and perversion. 1
Corinthians 6:19-20 says, "Do you not know that your bodies
are temples of the Holy Spirit, who is in you, whom you have
received from God? You are not your own; you were bought
at a price. Therefore, honor God with your bodies." I declare
that my body is the temple of the Holy Spirit, and I sever every
unholy connection with the spirit spouse. I break every sexual
bond that has been made in the spiritual realm, and I proclaim
that I am free from all sexual torment and impurity.

Declarations for the Key of Faith

1. Faith to Overcome Doubt and Fear

I declare that I am walking by faith and not by sight. 2 Corinthians 5:7 says, "For we live by faith, not by sight." I declare
that my faith in God is unwavering, and I will not be moved

by circumstances, fear, or doubt. The spirit of fear has no place in my life because I trust in the God who has called me to victory. I declare that my faith in Jesus Christ will silence every voice of doubt and insecurity, and I am fully confident in His promises.

2. Faith to Break the Spirit Spouse's Hold

I declare that by faith, I am breaking every bond and legal claim the spirit spouse has over my life. Matthew 17:20 says, "If you have faith as small as a mustard seed, you can say to this mountain, 'Move from here to there,' and it will move. Nothing will be impossible for you." I declare that my faith in Christ is powerful enough to move every spiritual mountain, including the stronghold of the spirit spouse. I command every demonic attachment to my life to be broken in the name of Jesus.

3. Faith to Be Strong and Courageous

I declare that I am strong and courageous. Joshua 1:9 says, "Have I not commanded you? Be strong and courageous. Do not be frightened, and do not be dismayed, for the Lord your God is with you wherever you go." I will not fear what lies ahead. I take bold steps of faith, even when I feel afraid. God is with me wherever I go, and I trust Him to lead, provide, and protect. I will do what He has called me to do without holding back.

4. Faith to Overcome the Spirit Spouse's Influence in My Life

I declare that no spirit spouse can dominate my life because my faith is rooted in the unshakable foundation of Christ. 1 John 5:4 says, "For everyone born of God overcomes the world. This is the victory that has overcome the world, even our faith." I declare that my faith in God gives me victory over every spirit spouse, every demonic influence, and every destructive force that seeks to hinder my life. I stand in the victory of Christ and declare that I am an overcomer.

5. Faith to Walk in God's Rest, Free from Spirit Spouse Torment

I declare that by faith, I am entering into God's rest and peace, free from the torment of the spirit spouse. Matthew 11:28-29 says, "Come to me, all you who are weary and burdened, and I will give you rest. Take my yoke upon you and learn from me, for I am gentle and humble in heart, and you will find rest for your souls." I declare that I am at peace and at rest in Christ. The spirit spouse can no longer disturb my peace, and I walk in the rest and security of God's presence.

Declarations for the Key of Freedom

1. Declaration of Freedom from All Spiritual Bondage

I declare that I am free in Christ Jesus. John 8:36 says, "So if the Son sets you free, you will be free indeed." I declare that every chain, every spiritual bondage, and every demonic stronghold in my life is broken today. The spirit spouse and any other unclean spirits have no legal right to bind me, for whom the Son sets free is truly free. I renounce all agreements with the spirit spouse, and I walk in the freedom Christ has purchased for me.

2. Declaration of Freedom to Get Married

I declare that I am free to be loved and to love. For it is written: "If the Son sets you free, you will be free indeed" (John 8:36). Therefore, I am free to get married, to stay married, and to thrive in a joyful, godly marriage. Every chain is broken, and I walk boldly into the promise of love and covenant.

3. Freedom to Pursue God's Will and Purpose for My Life

I declare that I am free to pursue God's will and purpose for my life. Romans 8:28 says, "And we know that in all things God works for the good of those who love Him, who have been called according to His purpose." I declare that no spirit spouse or demonic entity can hinder my God-given destiny. I am free to fulfill the unique plan that God has set before me, and I walk boldly in His will, knowing that I am fully equipped by His Spirit.

4. Freedom from the Spirit Spouse's Control Over My Finances

I declare that I am free from the spirit spouse's control over my finances. Deuteronomy 28:12 says, "The Lord will open the heavens, the storehouse of His bounty, to send rain on your land in season and to bless all the work of your hands." I decree that my financial blessings are no longer under the influence of any spirit spouse or demonic forces. I declare that my finances are blessed, and I receive prosperity from God, not from any demonic source. Every curse over my finances is broken in the name of Jesus.

5. Freedom from the Spirit Spouse's Influence Over My Emotions

I declare that I am free from the spirit spouse's manipulation of my emotions. Isaiah 26:3 says, "You will keep in perfect peace those whose minds are steadfast, because they trust in you." I declare that my emotions are under the control of the Holy Spirit. The spirit spouse no longer has the power to stir up confusion, jealousy, or anger in me. I walk in peace, joy, and emotional stability, free from the emotional manipulation of the enemy.

Practical Case Studies

Case Study 1: The Idol of Control through Health Anxiety

A woman tormented by fear of hospitals, illness, and losing control

Rooted in the Spirit Spouse

This isn't just anxiety. It's the fruit of a hidden covenant with a spirit spouse, a demonic counterfeit that has married her soul to fear and self-reliance.

This woman has unknowingly partnered with fear, building an altar of control to feel safe. But God desires to tear down this altar and invite her into grace.

Problem Summary

This woman is a believer who loves God but is tormented by fear, specifically manifesting as:

- ❖ White coat syndrome: fear of doctors, hospitals, and checkups. Her blood pressure spikes with anxiety.
- ❖ Extreme dietary restrictions: rigid eating patterns to avoid getting sick.
- ❖ Avoidance of hospitals, even when she's in pain.

- ❖ Obsessive online research about symptoms and health conditions.
- ❖ Prayers filled with panic: "Please, Lord, don't let me die. Don't let me be sick."
- ❖ Hidden belief: "God is good, but I'm not sure He'll protect my body."
- ❖ Increasing weakness despite health efforts because fear is feeding the problem

Root Issues

- ❖ Childhood trauma involving illness or watching a loved one suffer
- ❖ A fear of losing control, being vulnerable, or facing a scary diagnosis
- ❖ The deep-seated belief: "If I don't control this, no one will."

Stronghold Identified

The Idol of Control disguised as discipline and responsibility.

"If I eat clean, avoid hospitals, and watch every symptom, I can save myself."

But in truth, she's in bondage to fear.

The Key of Grace (Red)

Her breakthrough begins with the Key of Grace. Symbolized by the color red, representing the blood of Jesus. Grace breaks the lie that she must earn peace through control. Grace says

"You are safe, even when you're not in control."

And now, whenever she finds herself spiraling with fear or health panic, God invites her to look for red in her environment.

A red pillow.

A red flower.

A red pen.

A red light.

Let the color red become a holy pause, a visual reminder that the blood of Jesus speaks louder than the voice of fear.

"When you see red," the Lord says, "Remember: You are covered. Grace is stronger. You are mine."

Daily Grace Routine

Morning Reset

Repent:

"Lord, forgive me for putting trust in fear, routines, and self-discipline more than you. I surrender this idol of control and receive your grace."

Declare:

"I am not my own healer; Jesus is. My body is under covenant protection."

Scripture Meditation: My body prospers and is in good health even as my soul prospers (3 John 1:2)

Afternoon: Interrupt the Spiral:

"Fear does not own me. I trust the Lord, not symptoms. I trust God, not Google."

Breath + Scripture:

Inhale: "The Lord is my Shepherd…"

Exhale: "…I shall not want." (Psalm 23:1)

Visualize:

God's hand over her heart, her immune system, her blood pressure, and her doctor visits.

Evening Reset: Rest & Anchor

Lay Down Fear:

"Jesus, I give you every fear of sickness, death, and loss of control. I surrender to your healing power."

Create Atmosphere of Peace:

Light a candle. Play soft worship. Sit still in His presence.

Journal Victory:

"Today, I chose trust instead of fear when…"

Redemption Story

In time, she realizes this is not just anxiety, it's a spiritual covenant with fear, enforced by the spirit spouse. She repents, renounces the idol of control, and receives the Key of Grace. Her prayers become restful. Her body responds with peace, and she stops experiencing continuous infirmities. She eats to nourish, not to control. She enjoys life again. She now allows herself the occasional burger or slice of cake without fear.

She can go to a checkup calmly, because she is not her own protector, God is.

Case Study 2: The Idol of Security through Financial Anxiety

A man gripped by fear of lack and poverty.

Rooted in the Spirit Spouse

This isn't just stress over money. It's deeper. It's spiritual. A spirit spouse often mimics provision by convincing the soul that security comes from self not from God.

Problem Summary

This man is no longer struggling to make ends meet, he's stable. He has a good job, savings in the bank, and everything he once prayed for. But peace has not come.

- ❖ He feels guilty spending on himself for even simple things like a nice meal or vacation.
- ❖ He obsessively checks his accounts, tracking every transaction with dread.
- ❖ He hoards money, not out of greed but out of deep fear as if poverty is waiting just around the corner.
- ❖ When he gives, it's reluctant or transactional, not joyful or free.
- ❖ He doesn't feel safe, even though he has more than enough.
- ❖ He says "God is my provider" but lives like it's all up to him.
- ❖ Financial stability hasn't brought joy it's brought more pressure.

- ❖ He sometimes judges others who spend freely, masking his anxiety as wisdom.

Deep down, he's still afraid. Not of being broke but of losing control, of not having "enough" to be okay.

Root Issues

Grew up in a home where money was scarce or unstable

- ❖ Saw his parents argue or suffer over finances.
- ❖ Felt responsible too early for the family's wellbeing.
- ❖ Believes subconsciously: "If I don't earn it, I don't deserve it"

Stronghold Identified

The Idol of Security through Self-Provision

"If I enjoy my money, I might lose it"

"I must keep looking for new avenues to make more money because what if something happens to deplete what I have already accumulated"

"If I don't control every dollar I might lose it."

The Key of Faith

The Key of Faith is represented by the color orange. Like the rising sun that announces a fresh start. When fear tries to speak louder than trust, God invites him to look for orange as a holy reminder:

A traffic cone.

A sunset.

An orange pen.

A flame.

A tangerine on the table.

Orange means God sees the need and is already moving. "Look up. The pressure is not yours to carry."

Daily Faith Routine

Morning Routine:

1. Repent & Return to Trust

"Lord, I repent for clinging to control through my finances. I've trusted my budget more than your heart. Even though you've blessed me, I've lived as if I'm still in lack. I lay down fear, and I receive grace."

2. Declare Boldly

"I am not in survival mode, I am in Kingdom abundance. I have enough. God has provided, and I trust Him to provide again."

3. Scripture Meditation

"And my God shall supply all your need according to His riches in glory by Christ Jesus."

(Philippians 4:19)

Afternoon Practice:

1. Challenge the Scarcity Reflex

When you're tempted to obsess over saving, hoard money, or feel guilty for enjoying a small gift:

Say aloud: "My joy is not a threat to my security. My Father provides again and again."

2. Practice Breath + Scripture

Breathe deeply and say:

Inhale: "The Lord is my shepherd…"

Exhale: "…I shall not want." (Psalm 23:1)

3. Faith Trigger:

Look for something orange, a fruit, a candle, a piece of clothing and let it remind you that God's provision is available for you.

Evening Anchor: Embrace the Gift

1. Let Go of Scarcity Thinking

"God, I release the fear that something bad will happen if I enjoy what you've given. I break agreement with the lie that I must earn rest, joy, or comfort. I choose to receive today's provision with open hands and a grateful heart."

2. Embrace Joyful Stewardship

Ask yourself:

What is one small, life-giving way I can enjoy what I've been given today, without guilt, without fear?

Consider:

Ordering the meal you actually want

Giving spontaneously

Booking the trip, you've been putting off

3. Scripture Meditation

"Command those who are rich... not to trust in uncertain riches but in the living God, who gives us richly all things to enjoy." (1 Timothy 6:17)

Redemptive Breakthrough

As this man began applying the Key of Faith and breaking agreement with the idol of scarcity, something shifted. He stopped checking his bank app ten times a day. He bought his wife a gift without guilt. He gave to someone in need and felt joy instead of panicking. He started to receive money from unexpected sources and noticed that he was enjoying God's supernatural blessing of financial help. One evening, while sitting outside and watching the sunset, he noticed the orange sky. For the first time in a long time, he exhaled deeply and whispered, "I really am free." He now enjoys his provision without fear, because he trusts the Giver more than the gift.

LET'S STAY CONNECTED

- ❖ Visit my website: www.sharonbisha.com
- ❖ Join my prayer room by sending an email to sharonmbi@hotmail.com
- ❖ Follow me on Instagram: Sharon_mbi
- ❖ Follow me on TikTok: Sharonmbi4real
- ❖ Stream my deliverance music, including Seven Songs from Heaven, on: Spotify • Amazon Music • Apple Music • and all streaming platforms
- ❖ Watch teachings, testimonies, and prayer videos on YouTube @ Sharon Mbi

I host worship nights throughout the year, and a special annual worship night in Southern California called • Worship • War • Win. These powerful in-person gatherings are designed to help you encounter God and break spiritual bondages, especially the spirit spouse. Stay connected to my website and social media to know when and where these worship nights are happening so you can attend and experience your own breakthrough.

God bless you.